PANDA

成都，一座来了就不想离开的城市……

TO LIVE IN CHENGDU, NOT TO LEAVE.

ART GALLERY OF ALBERTA
Enterprise Square
10230 Jasper Avenue
Edmonton,Alberta,Canada

This publication was poduced to complement
an exhibition, organizedby the
Art Gallery of Alberta and the Chengdu
Profound Culture Promoting Co.,LTD.

Canada Council for the Arts
Conseil des Arts du Canada

THE CITY OF Edmonton

Alberta Foundation for the Arts

Art Gallery of Alberta
April 13-June 10,2007

ISBN:0-88950-144-0

Editor:Catherine Crowston
Design:Pamela Clark
Photography:Ximeng Zhang 张西蒙
Registrar: Fei Wu 吴 飞
Translator: Xiangbing Chen 陈先兵
Collator: Li Wang 王 莉
Printing:Chengdu Classic Design & Printing Co.,LTD.

No. 7 SW Fuqing Road
Chengdu, 610031
China
CHENGDU PROFOUND CULTURE PROMOTING CO.,LTD
成都厚重文化传播有限公司
地址：中国·四川·成都市抚琴西南路7号
电话：+86 28 87767926
传真：+86 28 87767506
策划：王孝明
邮箱：xiaoming677@sina.com

Wang Xiaoming, Director in Chief
Telephone: +86 28 87767926
Fax: +86 28 87767506
Email: xiaoming677@sina.com.cn

We extend our appreciation and thanks to-

Mr.Conglin Cheng, Consultant in Chief
艺术总顾问：程丛林

Chengdu Association of Cultural Industry
成都市文化产业协会

Chengdu International Nongyuan Artists Creating Centre
成都国际浓园艺术家创作基地

成都中嘉设计印务有限责任公司
CHENGDU CLASSIC DESIGN & PRINTING Co., Ltd.

『中国感觉 成都艺术』架起中加两国艺术之桥

每次展览背后都会有一个有趣的故事，无疑『中国感觉，成都艺术』展也不例外。2006年7月，受埃德蒙顿市市长办公室的中国业务主任Dick Wong先生邀请，我同到此访问的成都媒体以及该市领导会晤，讨论了未来在两市之间展开文化及商业交流。Dick Wong先生与中－加商务协会的Kirk Quan先生，成都日报集团的陈林先生和熊艳先生，成都市对外文化交流协会的黄强先生一行，拜访了阿尔伯塔艺术馆（AGA）。

我们的话题迅速的转到的成都丰富的文化遗产方面。最近，我为香港《中国亚洲艺术考古》杂志撰文，在文中详尽地谈到了三星堆文化。这是中国20世纪考古发掘的重大发现。我们的成都朋友盛情邀请我们，下次成都之行一定要去参观三星堆博物馆和成都周边其他的考古发现。仅隔几月，我受『加拿大国际文化促进了解基金会』邀请，参加了一个国际项目，旨在开拓中加两国博物馆之间的交流。由此，我决定在中国期间要拜会这几位成都朋友。

在成都，朋友们热情地接待了我，并陪同我造访了成都许多考古遗址，地方文化和宗教中心。后经朋友引见，我认识了成都厚重文化传播有限公司的王孝明先生，由此开始了我最有趣的行程。我们访问了40多位艺术家以及他们的创作室。从雕塑，绘画，到数码影像作品，其艺术的多样性和艺术成就都让我惊讶和兴奋不已。我的脑海中立刻打定了一个主意，要让他们的作品在阿尔伯塔艺术馆（AGA）展出。

我将有关成都艺术的照片资料带给AGA业务主任/副馆长凯瑟琳女士，她看了之后，『中国感觉，成都艺术』的准备工作由此拉开。经历几个月共同的作品筛选后，凯瑟琳于2007年1月，亲赴成都同王孝明先生共同完成最终的展出作品的确定。在她访蓉期间，得的到了成都市对外文化交流协会的黄强先生和成都外事办的司蓓蓓小姐，以及埃德蒙顿市市长办公室中国业务主任Dick Wong先生的热情帮助。

能够将中国这些具有创新精神和激励意志的艺术作品第一次引荐到北美地区，对阿尔伯塔艺术馆来说，机会难得，并深感荣誉。在此，我想谢意成都各方，特别是参加本次展出的作品的艺术家，感谢他们为我们提供了这次机会，向加拿大的人民打开了了解新中国和中国当代艺术家的窗口。

托尼 罗皮诺
阿尔伯塔艺术馆行政馆长
2007年3月

Building Bridges between Canada and China Through Art – China Sensation

The origin of an exhibition usually has an interesting story behind it and China Sensation certainly does. In July of 2006, Mr. Dick Wong, Director of China Initiatives for the City of Edmonton, invited me to meet with media and business leaders from the City of Chengdu in Edmonton to discuss future business exchanges between our the two cities. Mr. Kirk Quan of the China-Canada Business Association, Mr. Chen Lin of the Chengdu Daily News Group and Mr. Xiong Yan, Director, and Mr. Huang Qiang of the Chengdu Association for Cultural Exchange with Foreign Countries came with Dick Wong to the Art Gallery of Alberta (AGA).

Our discussions quickly turned to the rich cultural heritage of Chengdu. I had recently written a review of a book on Chinese Archaeology for Arts of Asia magazine in Hong Kong, in which I talked at length about Sanxindui, one of the most fascinating and rich archeological sites of China discovered in the 20th century. Our Chengdu friends kindly invited me to visit the Sanxingdu Museum and other archeological sites around Chengdu on my next visit to China. Just a few months later I was invited by the Canadian Fund for International Understanding through Culture to participate in an exchange program to open communication between museum directors in Canada and China. I decided to visit to my new friends in Chengdu while in China.

I was met by Mr. Huang Qiang and we explored the many archeological sites and wonderful cultural and religious centres in Chengdu. He introduced me to Mr. Wang Xiaoming of the Chengdu Profound Culture Promoting Co. Ltd. and I began the most interesting part of my trip. We visited at least forty artists in their studios. I was completely surprised and excited by the variety and quality of the artistic work being done in every medium from sculpture and painting to digital photography. There was no doubt in my mind that we had to exhibit this work at the AGA.

I showed Catherine Crowston, AGA Chief Curator and Deputy Director the photographs of the art from Chengdu and preparations for the China Sensation exhibition began. After working together for several months choosing the artists to include in the show, Catherine made a visit to Chengdu in January 2007 to make the final selection of works with the help of Wang Xiaoming. Catherine was also helped in her visit by the kind assistance of Huang Qiang and Ms. Si Beibei from the Chengdu Municipal Foreign Affairs Office and Dick Wong from the City of Edmonton.

It is a unique opportunity and a rare honour for the Art Gallery of Alberta to present such innovative and challenging works from China for the very first time in North America. I want to thank all of our collaborators in Chengdu and especially the artists in the exhibition for giving us the opportunity to open a window on the new China and its wonderfully experimental artists to the people of Canada.

Tony Luppino
Executive Director
Art Gallery of Alberta

中国感觉 成都艺术

『中国感觉，成都艺术』 的参展艺术作品主要来自成都的22位艺术家，成都是中国四川的省会城市。当今的中国正在积极发展和创新，中国当代艺术反映了中国社会变革中的挑战和激励。年轻艺术家正在不断的创造新的艺术形式，这不仅为中国艺术，也为世界艺术带来了新的理念。

『中国感觉,成都艺术』呈现了中国当今艺术创作本质的多面性。其中包含了成熟艺术家，从他们的作品中可以清晰的看到中国传统书法，风景，肖像等艺术形式的结合。年轻艺术家们的作品，更加敏锐和深刻地表现了中国的艺术革新，他们紧密连接西方当代艺术，并受其影响。他们展现出了对娱乐和媒体的深刻理解，对现代生活，对艺术创作的社会现实风格的意向和思想，作出了极有趣的精妙评论，而这种意象和思想，在中国社会变革的初期非常盛行。他们的作品或许表面看起来轻松，好玩，背后体现的是伴随世界高速发展和扩张中出现的另一面。 本次展出的独特性，在于突出表现了成都现实生活与悠久历史文化在社会中的矛盾冲突，因为『新』而让人对其饶有兴趣。『中国感觉』，是一次难得机会，去发现来自新的，并不断发展的中国的艺术家们的作品吧。

我们要感谢成都厚重文化传播有限公司的王孝明先生及其工作人员，同我们一同策展，甄选艺术家及其作品，并安排到加拿大展出作品的运输。他们完成展览画册的制作，为我们提供了对艺术家及其作品的概况。我们同样要感谢阿尔伯塔艺术馆的工作人员：Clint Wilson （高级筹备员），Duncan Johnson（筹备员）, Bruce Dunbar（注册师），Pamela Clark（助理注册师），感谢他们为本次展出所作的筹备和文件制作工作。

凯瑟琳 克劳斯顿
业务主任/副馆长

CHINA SENSATION New Art from Chengdu

CHINA SENSATION : New Art from Chengdu features the work of 22 artists from Chengdu, the capital city of Sichuan, in the People's Republic of China. There is a spirit of boldness and innovation in China today, and contemporary Chinese art reflects the unique challenges and excitement of its changing society. Young Chinese artists are fostering a new and revolutionary form of art, one that is bringing new ideas and new images to the art world - both within and outside the country.

CHINA SENSATION represents the multi-dimensional nature of artistic production in China today. It includes works by a senior generation of artists, whose aesthetic concerns can be clearly linked to age-old traditions of art and image-making, to landscape painting and calligraphic drawing. The younger artists in the exhibition, point more keenly toward a new China and how it is inextricably linked to and influenced by the West. They demonstrate a keen knowledge of entertainment and media and offer often ironic and subtle critiques of modern life and the imagery and ideology of the social realist style of art-making that was prevalent in China during the early days of the revolution. Their work might often appear light-hearted and playful, yet they also present the flip-side of progress which often comes with growth and expansion.

What is unique to this exhibition is the strong presence and reality of living in China today - the paradox of a society steeped in history, yet striving to be "new." **CHINA SENSATION** is a unique opportunity to see the work of artists from a new and ever evolving China.

We would like to thank Mr. Wang Xiaoming and the staff of the Chengdu Profound Culture Promoting Co. Ltd for working with us on planning the exhibition, making the selection of artists and works and for arranging to have the exhibition shipped to Canada. They also oversaw the production of this exhibition catalogue, which provides a comprehensive overview of the artists and their works of art. We are also very grateful to the staff of the Art Gallery of Alberta: Clint Wilson, Senior Preparator; Duncan Johnson, Preparator; Bruce Dunbar, Registrar and Pamela Clark, Assistant Registrar for all their work on preparing and documenting the work for exhibition.

Catherine Crowston
Deputy Director / Chief Curator

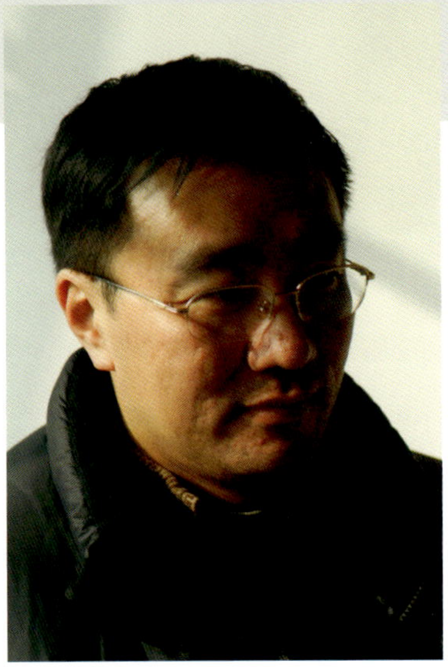

1963 Born in Chengdu, China
1986 Graduated from Sichuan Fine Arts Institute.
Currently Associate Professor in Fine Arts Department, Sichuan College of Education

Solo Exhibitions

1993 Solo Exhibition of Yang Cao, China National Art Museum, Beijing, China
2002 “The Vanished Space”, Chengdu Contemporary Art Gallery, Chengdu
2003 “The Vanished Space”, Tao Water Art Gallery, USA
2005 “The Lost Memories”, Tao Water Art Gallery, USA

Group Exhibitions

1989 Fine Arts Exhibition of 40th Anniversary of PRC, Sichuan Art Museum, Chengdu, China (Bronze Medal winner)
1992 1990s Fine Arts Biennial in Guangzhou, Guangzhou (Prize for Excellence winner)
1992 Contemporary Fine Arts Exhibition of China, Hong Kong Arts Centre, Hong Kong
1993 Oil Painting Exhibition of Chengdu, China National Art Museum, Beijing
1997 “Pufa” Contemporary Fine Arts Exhibition of China, Shanghai Art Museum, Shanghai
1999 100 Sichuan Artists Oil Painting Exhibition within A Century, Chengdu Arts Centre, Chengdu
1999 Fine Arts Exhibition of 50th Anniversary of PRC, Sichuan Art Museum, Chengdu, China
2001 “The Sichuan Link”, Bcexham Gallery, London, Britain
2003 “Hand in Hand in the New Century” 3rd China National Oil Painting Exhibition, China National Art Museum, Beijing, China

一九六三年九月生于中国成都。一九八六年毕业于四川美术学院油画系。
现为四川教育学院美术系副教授。

个展：

一九九三年在中国美术馆举办个人画展。中国北京
二〇〇二年在成都现代艺术馆举办『消失的空间』个人油画展。
二〇〇三年在美国Tao Water Art Gallery 举办『The Vanished Space』个人画展。
二〇〇五在美国Tao Water Art Gallery 举办『The Lost Memories』个人画展。

展览：

一九八九年参加在四川美术馆举办的庆祝建国四十周年四川省美术作品展。
一九九二年参加广州九十年代艺术双年展，获优秀作品提名奖。
一九九二年参加在香港艺术中心举办的中国当代油画精品展。
一九九三年参加在四川美术馆举办的四川油画展。
一九九六年参加在北京中国美术馆举办的成都油画展。
一九九七年参加在上海美术馆举办的九七浦发中国当代油画精品展。
一九九九年参加在四川美术馆举办的庆祝建国五十周年四川省美术作品展，获铜奖。
一九九九年参加在成都艺术中心举办的『天府百年百人中国油画展』。
二〇〇一年参加在英国 伦敦BCEXHAM GALLERIES举办的THE SICHUAN LINK画展。
二〇〇三年参加在北京 中国美术馆举办的『携手新世纪 第三届中国油画展』。

Yang Cao

曹阳

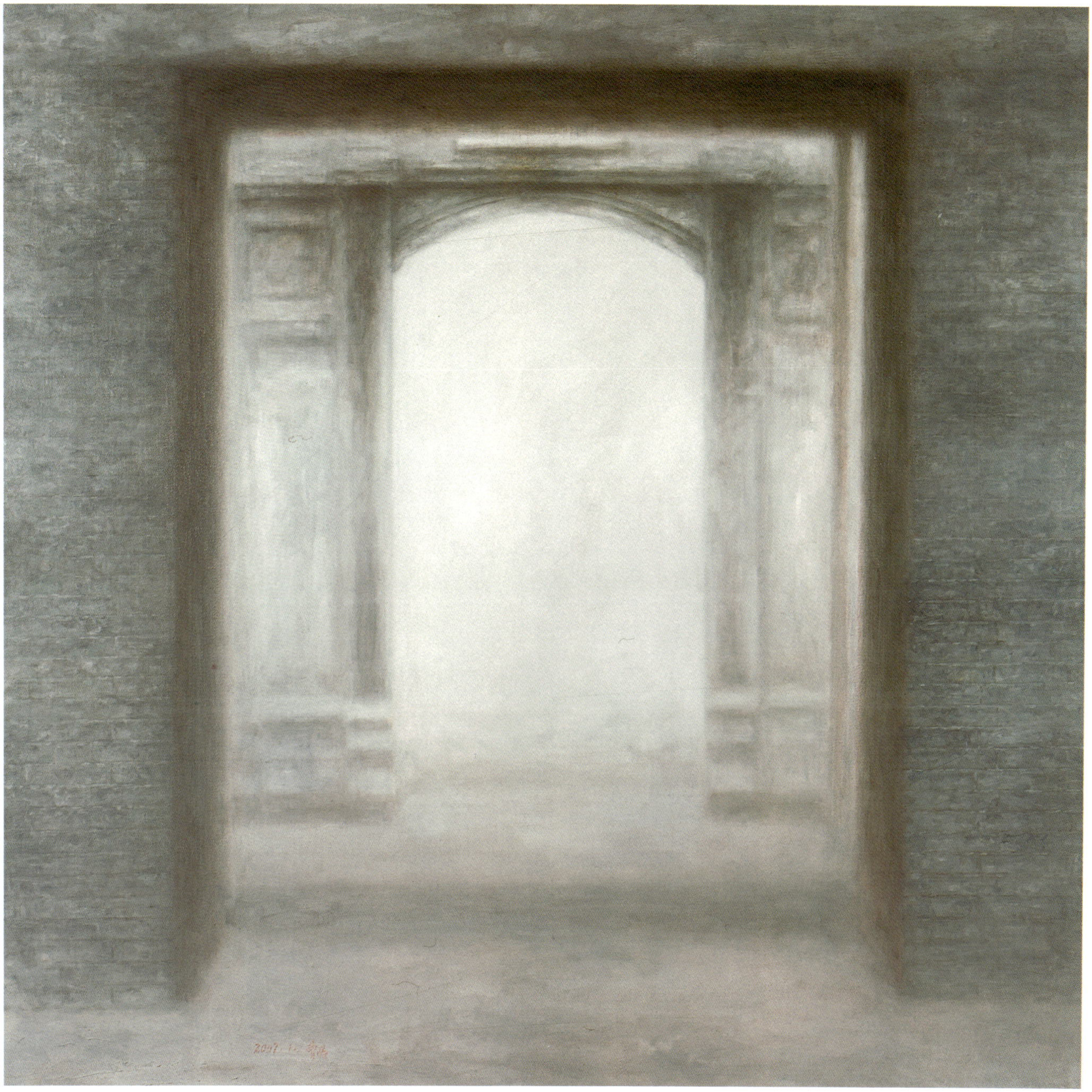

布面油画
《门影35》

The vision of the Doors NO.35
Oil on canvas
120cm×120cm

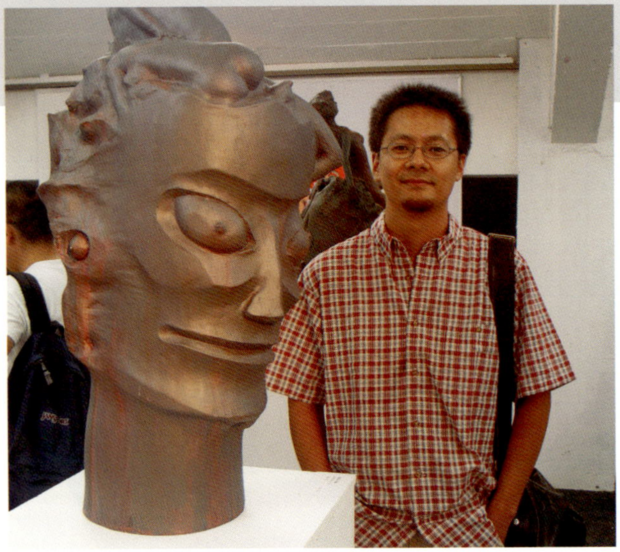

1973 Born in Chongqing, China
1998 Graduated from Sculpture Department of Sichuan Fine Arts Institute
Currently teaches in Architecture Institute of Southwest Jiaotong University
Member of China Sculptors Association
Professional Artist in Blue House Art Center

Works and Exhibitions

1997 4th China National Sport Fine Arts Show
Rainbow was awarded with a Bronze Medal
1999 The Fine Arts Exhibition of 50th Anniversary of PRC
Trees awarded with a Prize for Excellence in Sichuan Area.
2001 "Hover" and "Struggle" attended 5th China National Sport Fine Arts Show
2001 Sichuan Contemporary Sculpture Exhibition,Chengdu
2003 Sichuan Contemporary Sculpture Exhibition, Chengdu
2004 "The Mountain Villager" attended 10th China National Fine Arts Exhibition
2006 "The Outflow of the Souls" series attended 1st "New Power · China" Contemporary Art Biennale in Shanghai
2006 "The Wind over the Ice" attended China 2008 Olympics Sculpture Scene Exhibition and 6th China National Sport Fine Arts Show.

一九七三年8月出生于中国重庆
一九九八年毕业于四川美术学院雕塑系
现任教于西南交通大学建筑学院
中国雕塑学会会员

主要展览：

一九九七年雕塑《虹》获第四届中国体育美术展览 铜奖
一九九九年雕塑《树》参加建国五十周年美术展览 四川省美术作品·优秀奖
二〇〇一年雕塑《博》入选参加中国第五届体育美术展览
二〇〇一年雕塑《翔》入选参加中国第五届体育美术展览.
二〇〇三四川雕塑现状展览
二〇〇四年雕塑《山里人》入选中国十届美术展览
二〇〇六年雕塑《冰上的风》入选参加中国第六届体育美术展览 四川省美术作品·优秀奖
二〇〇六年雕塑《冰上的风》入选中国2008奥运会景观雕塑展览
二〇〇六年雕塑《出窍》系列入选参加上海首届『新动力·中国』当代艺术双年展

Xiang Cheng

程翔

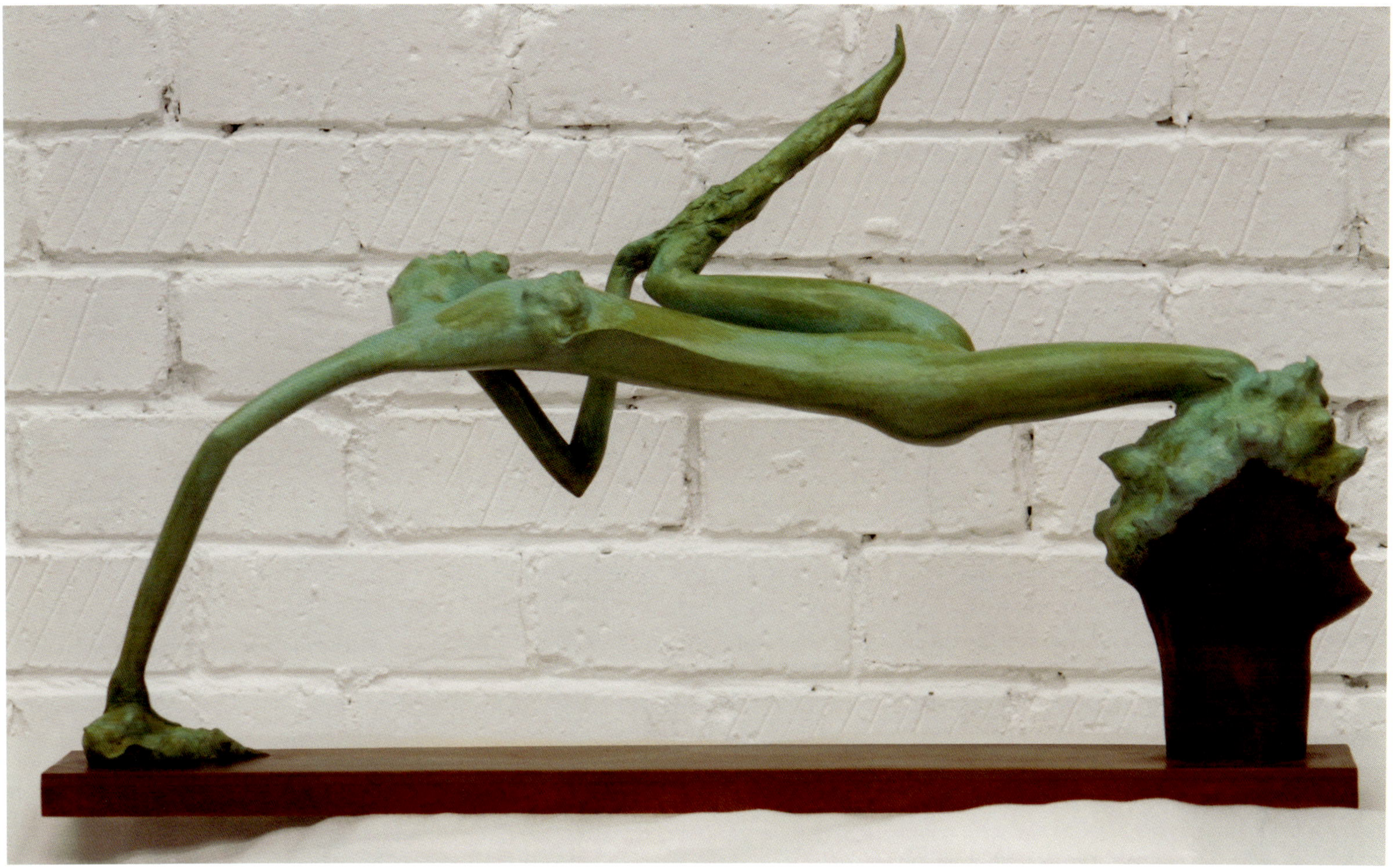

雕塑《出窍》

The Outflow of the Souls
Bronze
L:90cm W:22cm H:50cm

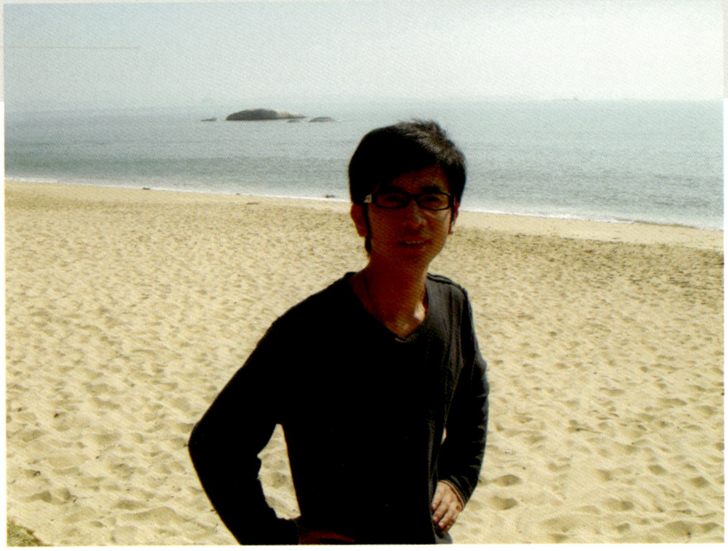

1992 Graduated from Fujian Industrial Arts School
1996 Graduated from China Central Industrial Arts College
Currently member of China Sculptors Association
Director of the Ceramic Committee of Sichuan Artists Association
Former Chairman of Ceramists Association of Dehua
2002 Established Chenshuo Atelier in Chengdu

Exhibitions

1999 Opera and resume were Selected in the CD of "109 Ceramists from the Mainland, Taiwan and Hong Kong of China"
2000 National Excellent Ceramic Competing Exhibition, Shanghai, China
The opus of Ares was awarded with a Prize for Excellence.
2000 Tsinghua University International Ceramic Exhibition in 2000, China National Art Museum, Beijing, China
The opus of Ares was collected by Tsinghua University.
2001 1st China Ceramics Exhibition, Beijing, China
The opus of State was awarded with a Prize for Excellence.
2002 "The Romantic Feeling of West China" Ceramic Exhibition, Chengdu, China
2006 1st "New Power • China" Contemporary Art Biennial, Yuan Gong Art Gallery, Shanghai, China

一九九二年毕业于福建工艺美术学校
一九九六年毕业于中央工艺美术学院
中国雕塑学会会员
四川美术家协会陶艺专委会理事
原德化陶艺家协会会长
二〇〇二年在成都建立『陈硕工作室』

展览：

一九九九年作品及简历编入《中国当代陶艺家大陆、台湾、香港109位》光盘
二〇〇〇年参加『全国优秀陶艺评比展』作品《战神》获优秀奖 中国上海
二〇〇〇年参加『2000年清华大学国际陶艺展』作品《战神》被清华大学收藏 中国美术馆
二〇〇一年参加『首届中国陶艺展』作品《形态》获优秀奖 中国北京
二〇〇二年参加『中国西部情雕塑展』 中国成都
二〇〇六年参加首届『新动力・中国』当代艺术双年展 中国上海原弓美术馆

Shuo Chen

陈硕

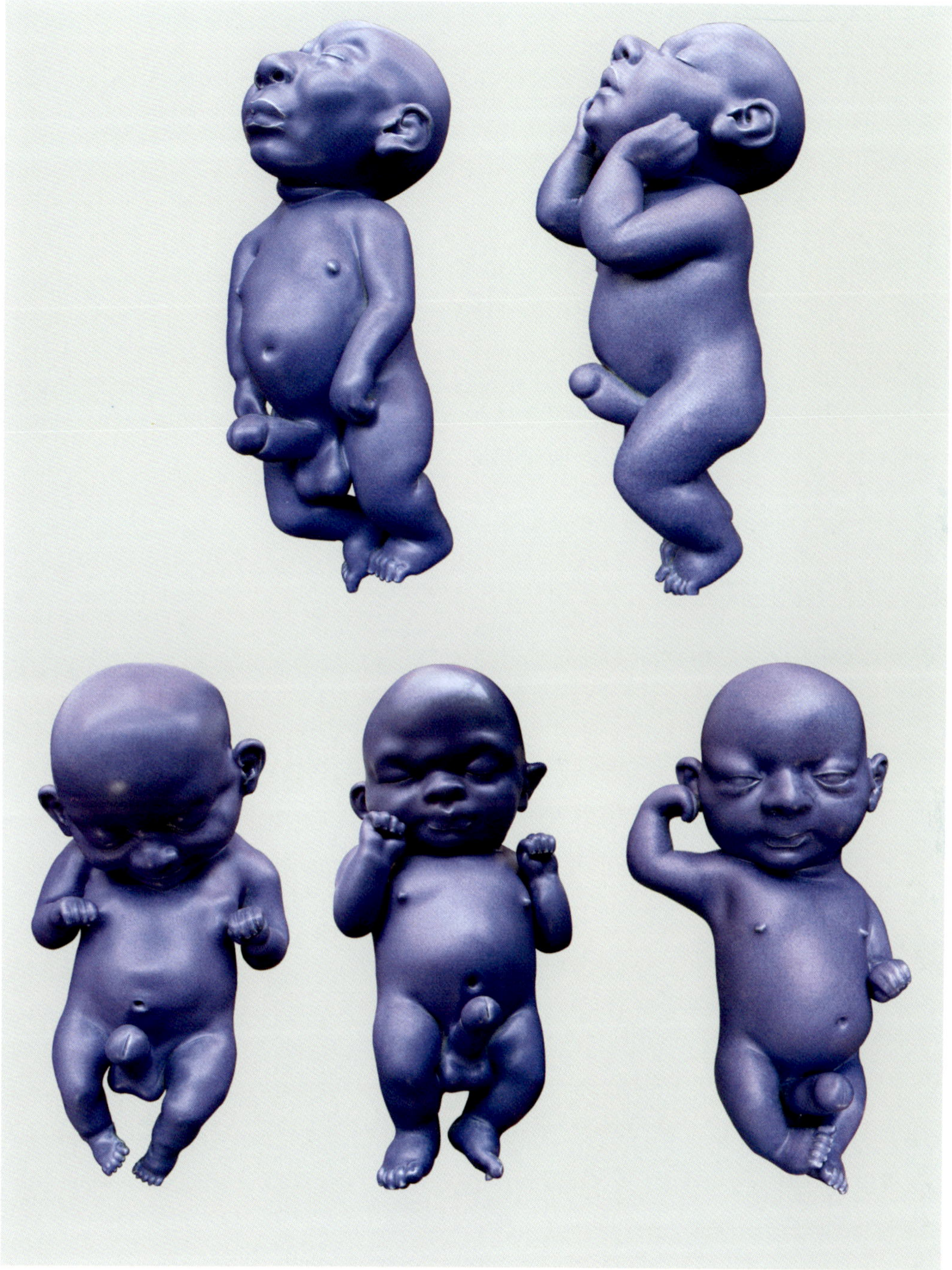

雕塑《快速发展-婴儿系列》

The Fast Development- Baby Series
Ceramic
L:32.5cm W:18cm H:9.4cm

一九六三年生于中国成都
一九九〇年毕业于四川美术学院版画系，现工作、生活在成都。

主要展览：

二〇〇二年 成都油画精品展览
二〇〇三年 四川『寻找』高校艺术巡回展览
二〇〇四年『错轨・并轨』成都东站艺术工作室开放展
二〇〇六年《首届(二〇〇六)『新动力・中国』当代艺术双年展》

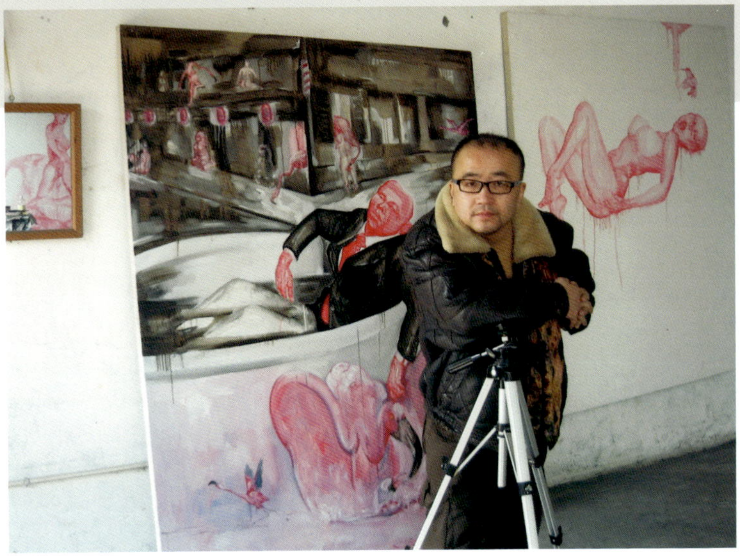

1963 Born in Chengdu, China
1990 Graduated from Print Department of Sichuan Fine Arts Institute
Currently lives and works in Chengdu

Exhibitions

2003 Seeking College Arts Tour Exhibition in Sichuan
2004 Public Show at East Station Art Studio
2006 1st New Power China Contemporary Art Biennale, Shanghai

Yi Diao

刁毅

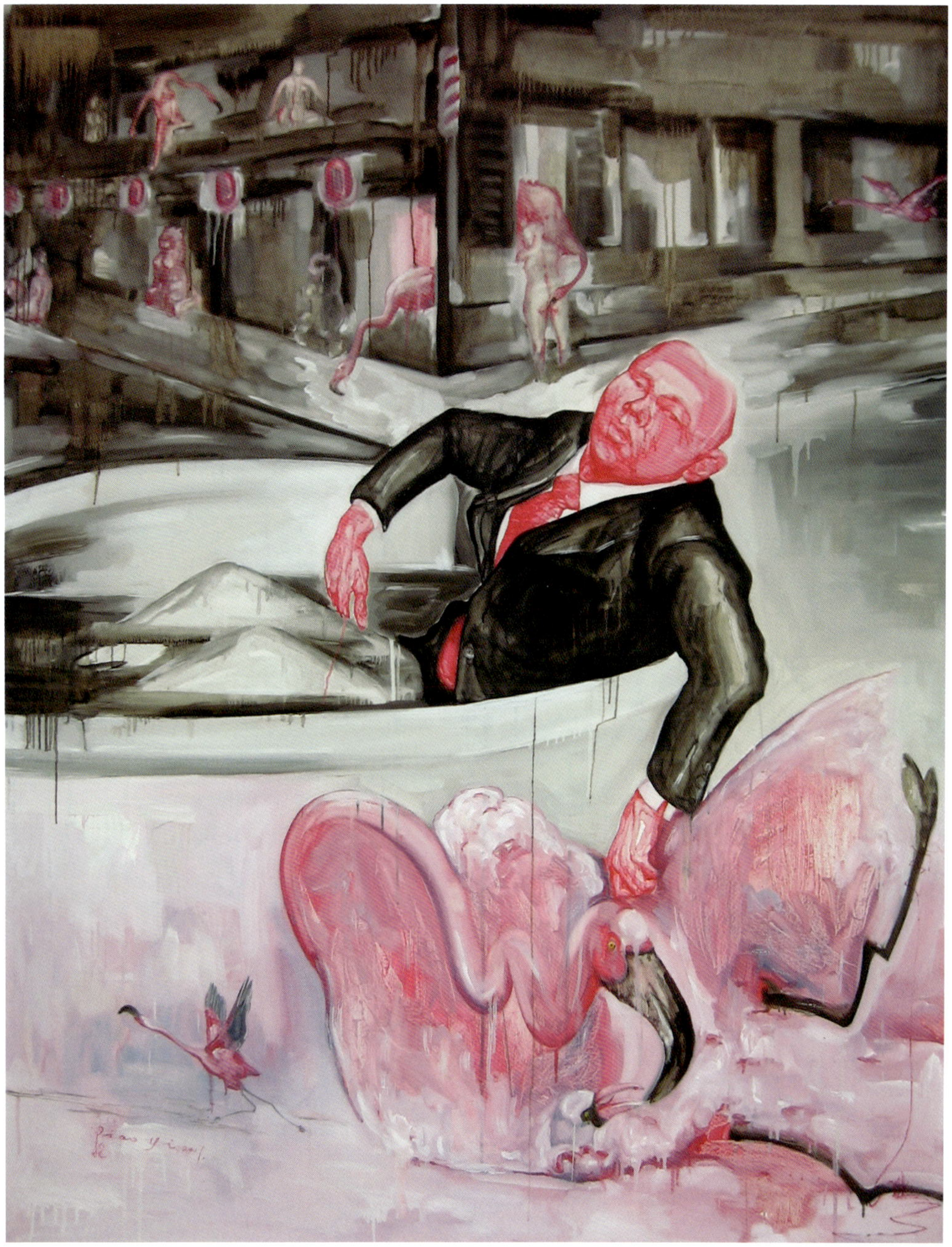

布面油画《夜宴1》

Night Banquet1
Oil on canvas
150cm×200cm

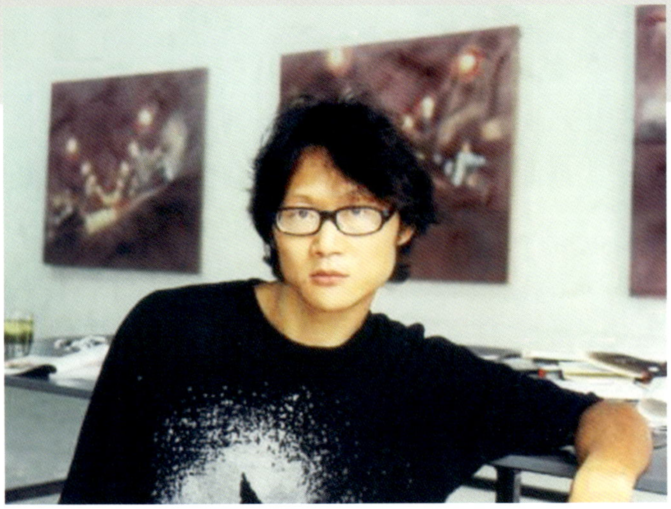

1968 Born in Sichuan, China
1992 Graduated from Sichuan Fine Arts Institute
Currently lives in Beijing and Chengdu

Solo Exhibitions

2002 "Street Light" Exhibition of Paintings by Qing Han, Canvas International Art Gallery, Amsterdam, the Netherlands
2004 "Under the Light" Solo Exhibition of Qing Han, Orient Foundation Macau---China Delegation, Macau, China
2006 "At Night" Art Exhibition, Red Gate Gallery, Beijing, China

Group Exhibitions

1999 "The Twinkling" Chinese Fine Arts at the End of the 20th Century, The David and Alfred Smart Art Museum, University of Chicago, U.S.A
2001 2001Chengdu Contemporary Art Exhibition, Chengdu, China
2003 3rd China National Oil Painting Exhibition, China National Art Museum, Beijing
2004 Art Rotterdam, Rotterdam, the Netherlands
2004 "Crowds and Voids: 11+1" Fine Arts Exhibition, Art Scene Warehouse, Shanghai
2004 KunstRAI2004, Amsterdam, the Netherlands
2005 18 Chinese Contemporary Artists "Living in Chengdu" Fine Arts Exhibition, Soobin Art Gallery, Singapore
2005 Exhibition Colectiva de an Rtistas - galeria 57, Portugal
2005 Representation Art Exhibition, Colectiva, S.Paulo, Brazil
2005 China Contemporary Art in 2005, Esquina con Colima. Col. Roma. Mexico
2006 China International Gallery Fair, Beijing, China

Public Collections:

AKZO NOBEL Art Foundation, the Netherlands
Orient Foundation----Macau, China

一九六八年生于中国四川
一九九二年毕业于四川美术学院

主要个展

二〇〇二年『街灯』Canvas international art 荷兰阿姆斯特丹
二〇〇四年『在灯光下』东方基金会中国代表处 中国澳门
二〇〇六年『在夜里』北京红门画廊 中国北京

主要群展

一九九九年『瞬间——二十世纪末的中国艺术』 美国芝加哥大学艺术博物馆
二〇〇一年成都当代艺术汇展 中国成都
二〇〇三年第三届中国油画展 中国美术馆
二〇〇四年鹿特丹国际艺术博览会 荷兰鹿特丹
二〇〇四年『喧嚣与空灵』11+1艺术景仓库 中国上海
二〇〇四年KunstRAI二〇〇四阿姆斯特丹国际艺术博览会 荷兰阿姆斯特丹
二〇〇五年『一八当代艺术家居住在成都』 新加坡斯民艺苑
二〇〇五年五七画廊艺术家联展 葡萄牙57画廊
二〇〇五年『有代表性的艺术展』 巴西圣保罗
二〇〇五年『中国当代艺术二〇〇五』 墨西哥
二〇〇六年中国国际画廊博览会 中国北京国际贸易展览中心

公共收藏

荷兰AKZO NOBEL艺术基金会
葡萄牙东方基金会

Qing Han

韩情

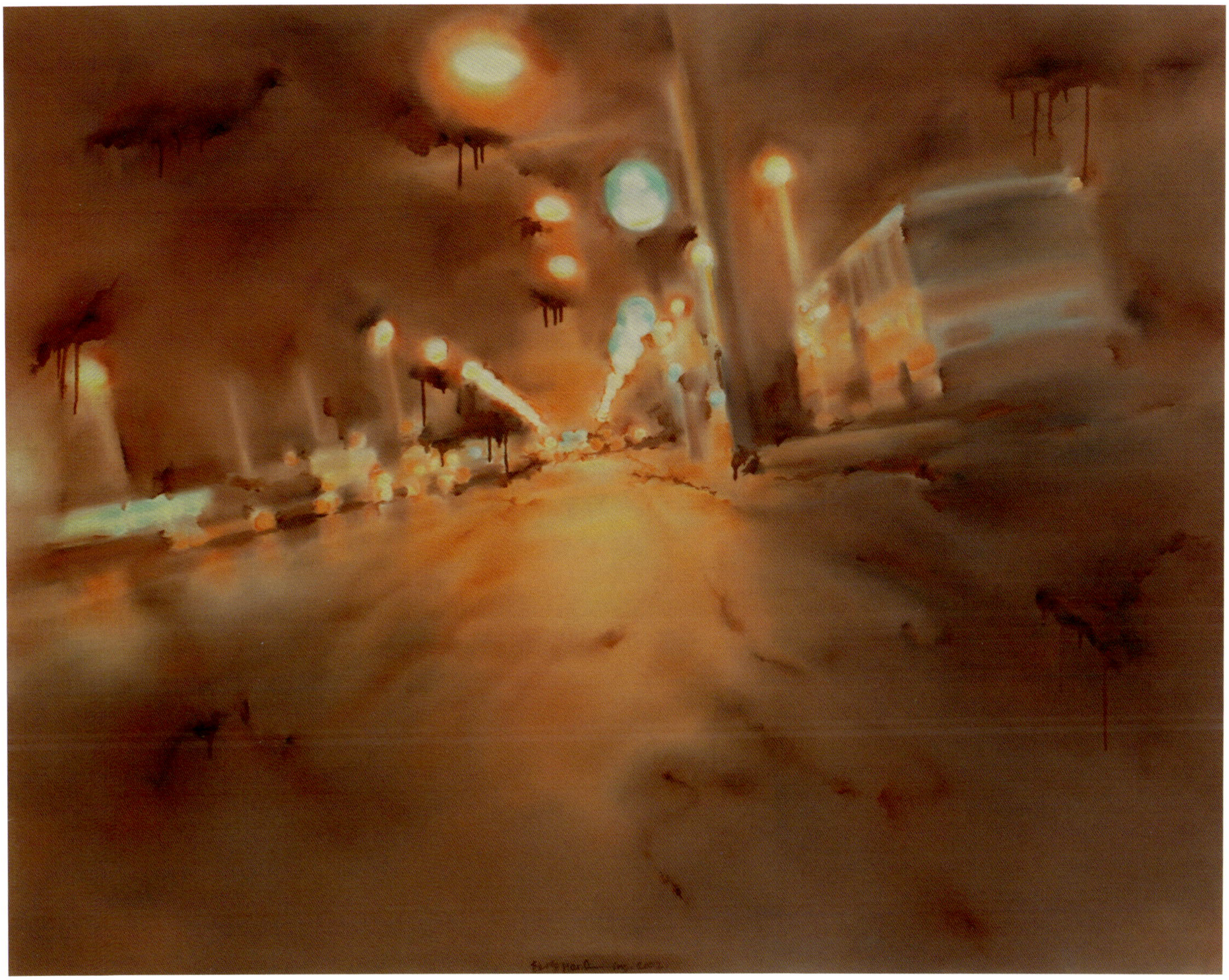

布面油画
《街灯2002 NO.12》

Street Lights 2002 NO.12
Oil on canvas
145cm×115cm

一九五八年10月生于中国四川
一九八七年毕业于四川美术学院绘画系
中国美术家协会会员

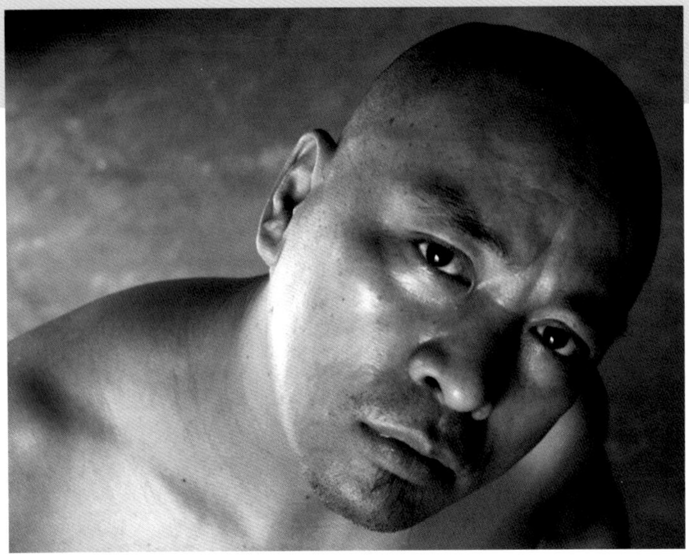

1958 Born in Sichuan, China
1987 Graduated from Sichuan Fine Arts Institute with a major in Oil Painting
Member of China Artists Association

Mingjin Huang

黄明进

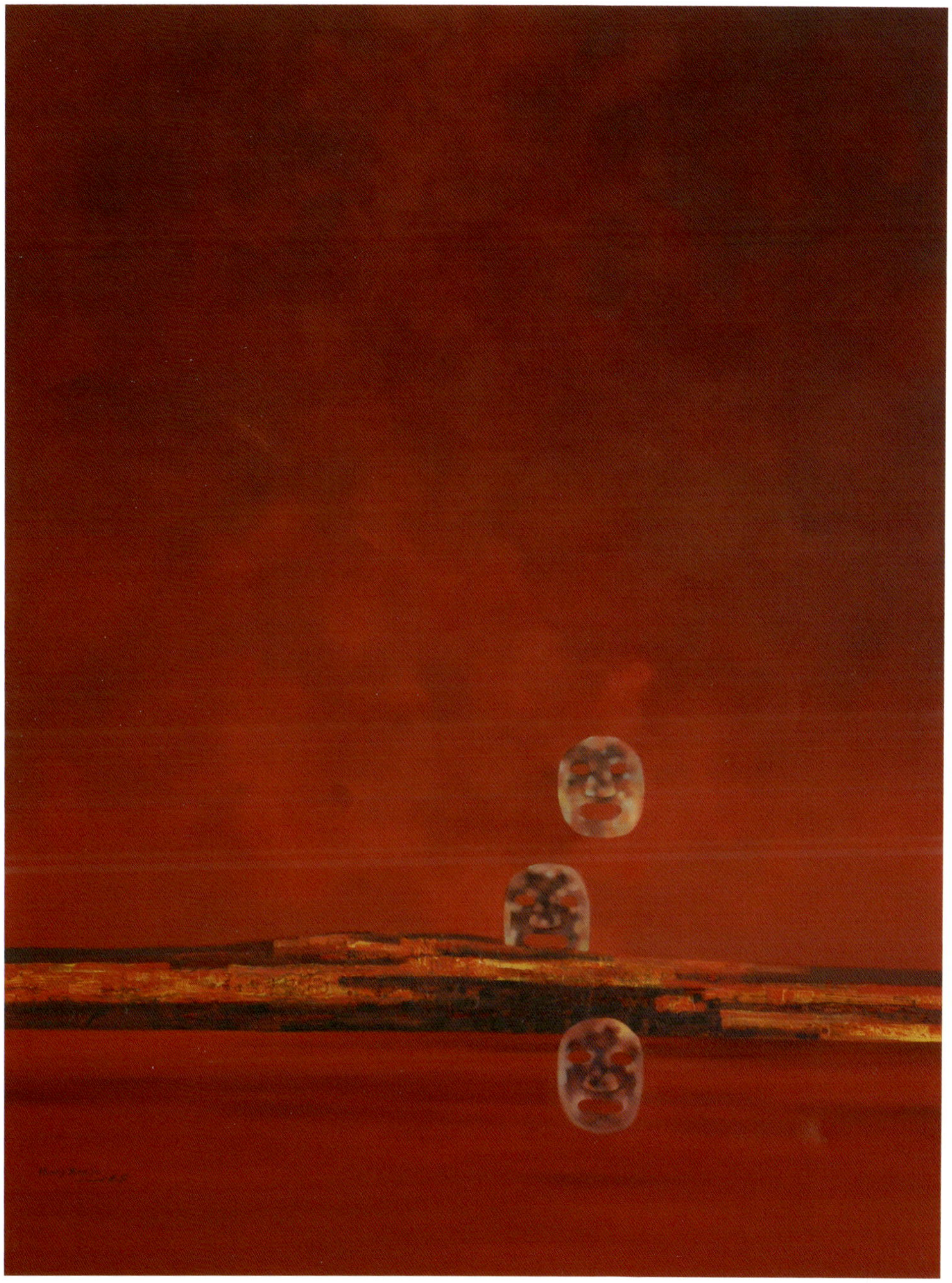

布面油画

《在·不在10》

To be or not to be NO.10
Oil on canvas
200cm × 150cm

生于中国南充，毕业于四川美术学院
二〇〇六在成都浓园建立艺术工作室

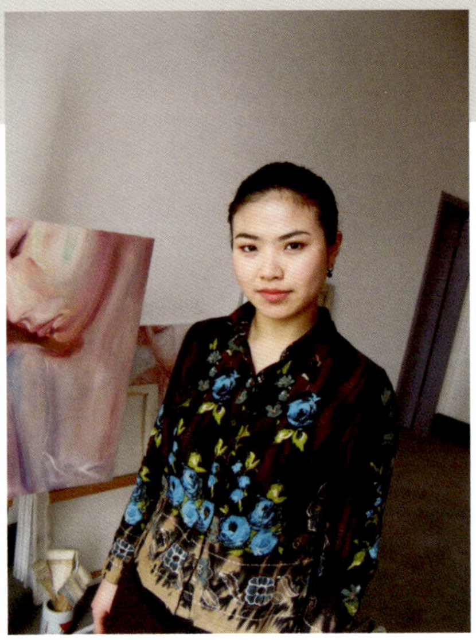

Born in Sichuan， China
Graduated from Sichuan Fine Arts Institute
2006 Set up her studio at Chengdu International Nongyuan Artists Creating Centre

Jing Jiang

蒋晶

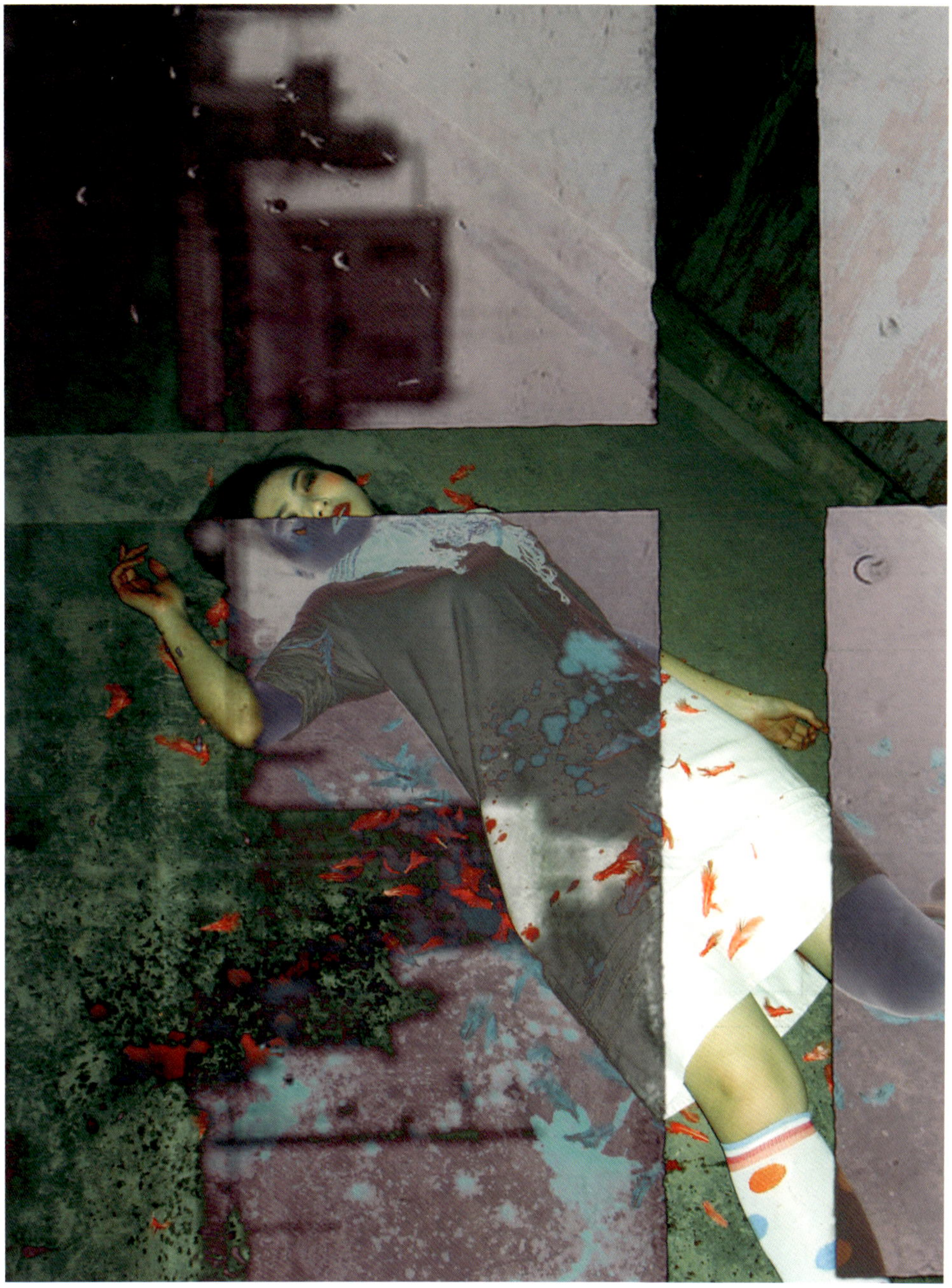

图像《遗忘时光》

The Lost Time and Space series
Photograph
100cm × 75cm

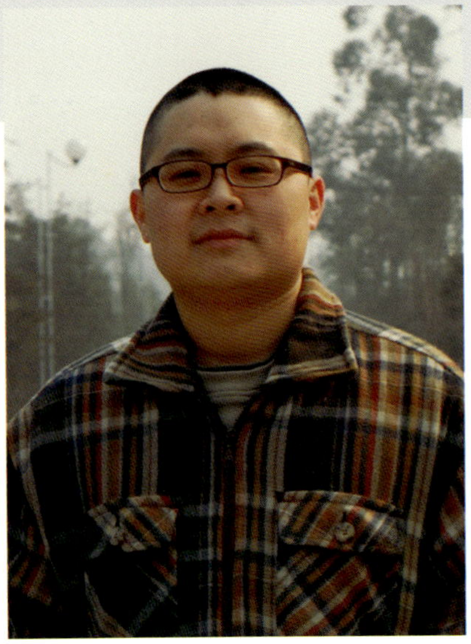

一九七六年生于中国成都
一九九九年毕业于四川美术学院版画系
一九九九年至今就职于成都商报社

1976 Born in Chengdu, China
1999 Graduated from Print Department, Sichuan Fine Arts Institute
Currently works for Chengdu Commercial Newspaper Group

Peng Jiang

蒋鹏

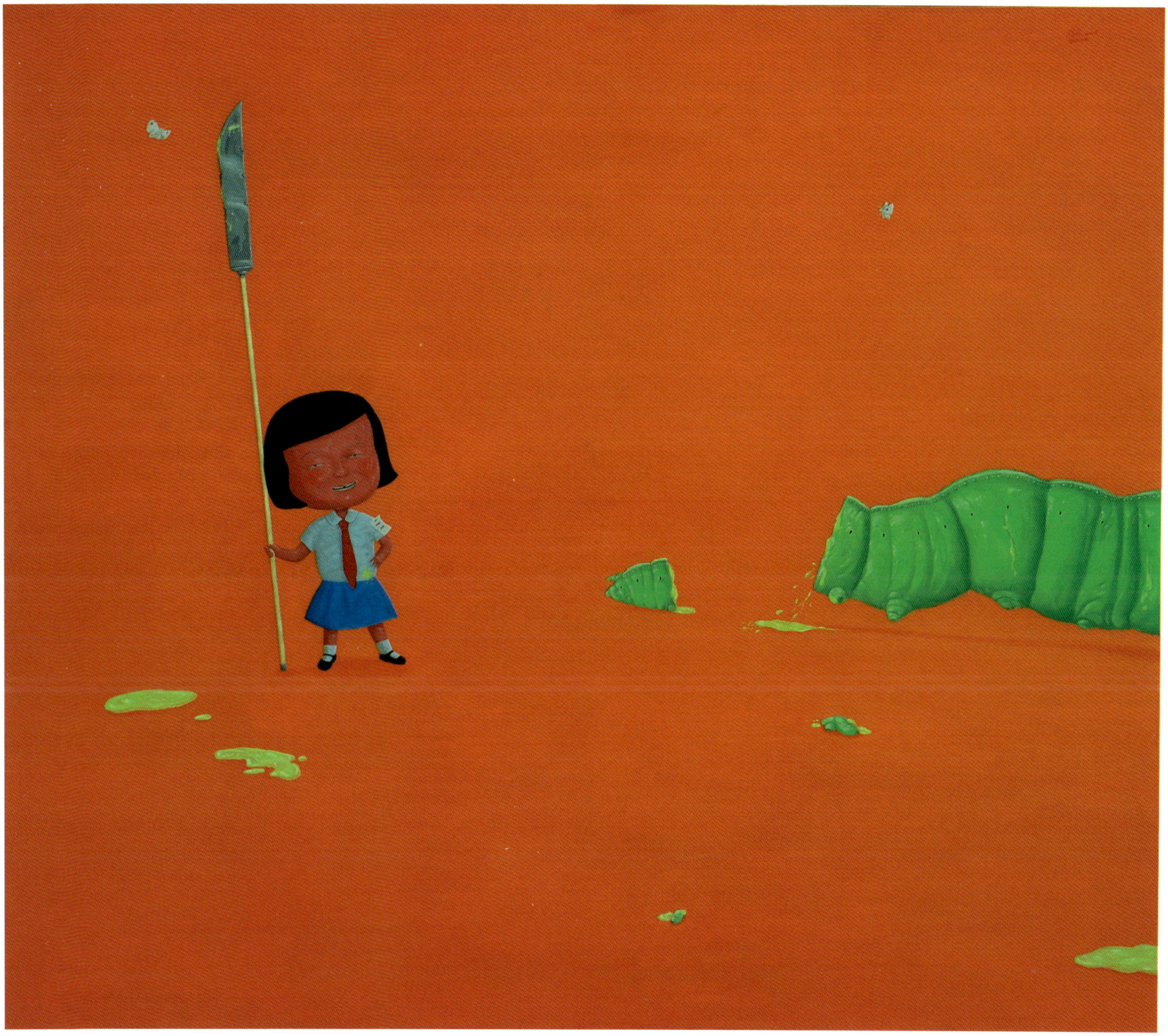

布面油画
《消灭一切害虫3》

Kill all the Pests 3
Oil on canvas
170cm×150cm

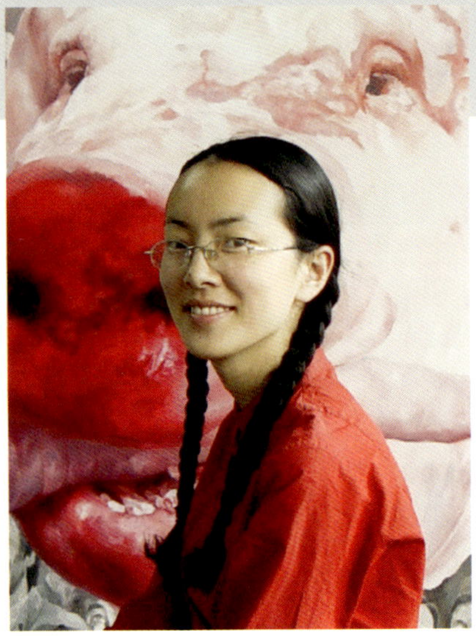

一九八〇年八月生于中国四川
二〇〇二年毕业于四川教育学院美术系
二〇〇五年九月至今，四川大学攻读油画硕士学位

主要展览：

二〇〇二年『链接·未来印象展』 成都现代艺术馆
『第二届四川青年美术作品展』 四川美术馆
二〇〇六年『四川大学二〇〇六春季艺术沙龙展』 四川大学美术馆

收藏：

成都现代艺术馆

1980 Born in Sichuan, China
2002 Graduated from Fine Arts Department, Sichuan College of Education
Currently studies in Sichuan University for a Master's Degree in Oil Painting

Exhibitions

2002 "Link · Future Impression", Chengdu Contemporary Art Museum, Chengdu
2002 2nd Sichuan Youth Fine Arts Exhibition, Sichuan Art Museum, Chengdu
2006 Spring Salon Exhibition of Sichuan University, Sichuan University Art Museum, Chengdu

Collected by

Chengdu Contemporary Art Museum

Mao Li

李貌

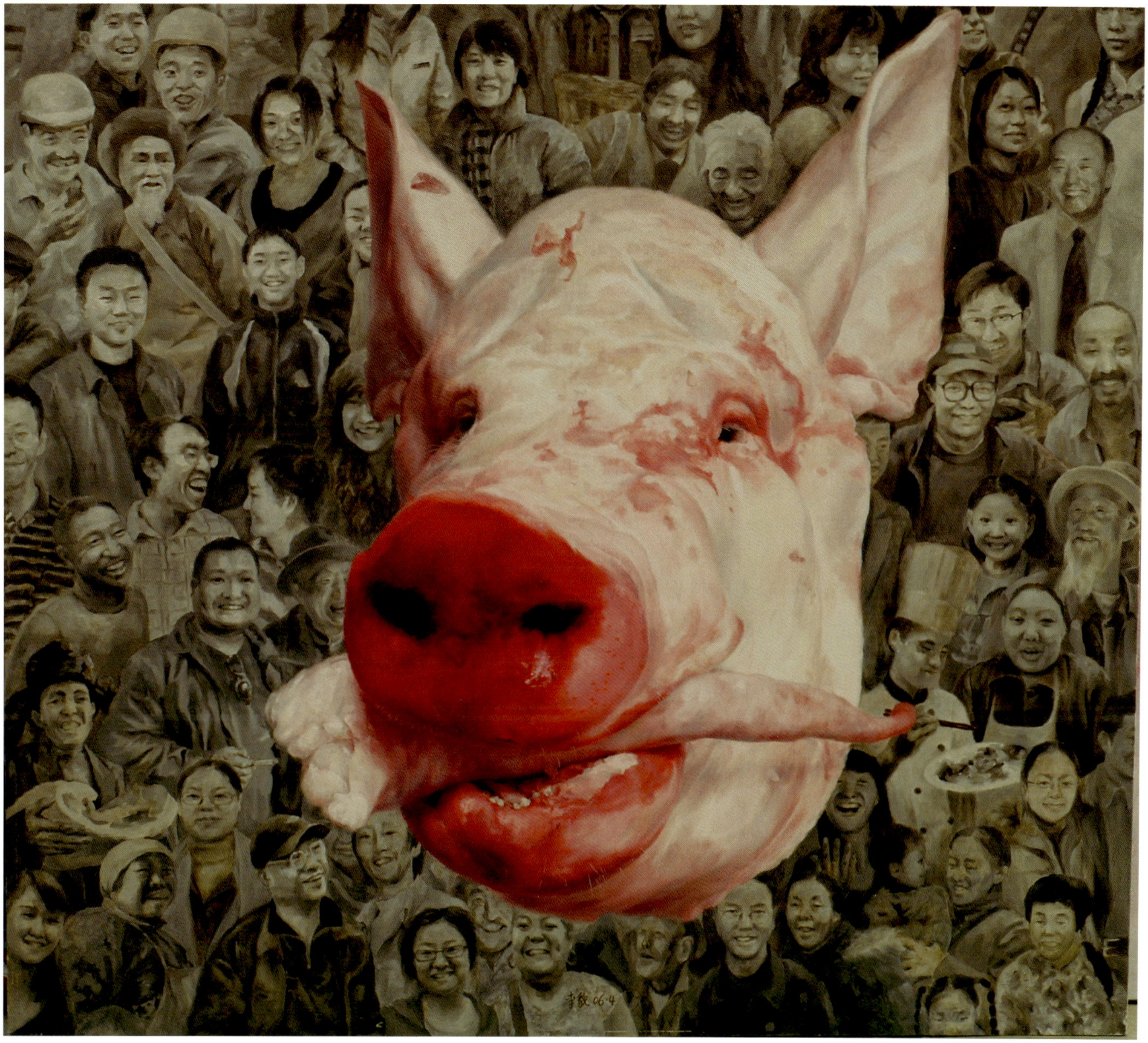

《见惯不惊》
布面油画

Confronting Without Excitement
Oil on canvas
170cm×155cm

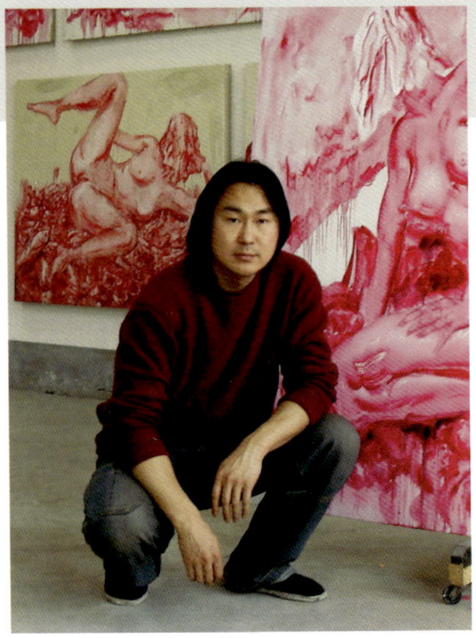

1969 Born in Hebei，China

1992 Graduated from Art Department, Leshan Fine Arts Institute with a major in Oil Painting

1998 Completed Advanced Course on Oil Painting from Sichuan Fine Arts Institute

Exhibitions

1999 Sichuan Oil Painting Treasure Exhibition, Chengdu, China

2001 Ya’ an Four Persons’ Art Exhibition, Chengdu, China

2002 Discovery Experimental Art Show, Chengdu, China

2003 National Youth Art Exhibition, Beijing, China

2006 1st “New Power · China” Contemporary Art Biennale, Shanghai, China

2006 “Not obedient” Seven Persons’ Exhibition, Beijing, China

2006 “Spring Sand” Art Exhibition, Chengdu, China

一九六九年四月八日生于中国河北保定

一九九二年毕业于乐山师范学院美术系油画专业

一九九八年结业于四川美术学院油画进修班

展览

一九九九年 『四川精品油画展』 中国成都

『四川美术作品大展』 中国成都

『巴蜀大地山水风景画大展』 中国成都

二〇〇一年 『雅安四人油画展』 中国成都

二〇〇二年 『"寻找"实验艺术展』 中国成都

二〇〇三年 『全国青年油画展』 中国北京

二〇〇六年 『春沙展』 中国成都

『"不乖"七人联展』 中国北京

『首届(二〇〇六)"新动力·中国"当代艺术双年展』 中国上海

Xueming Lian

廉学洺

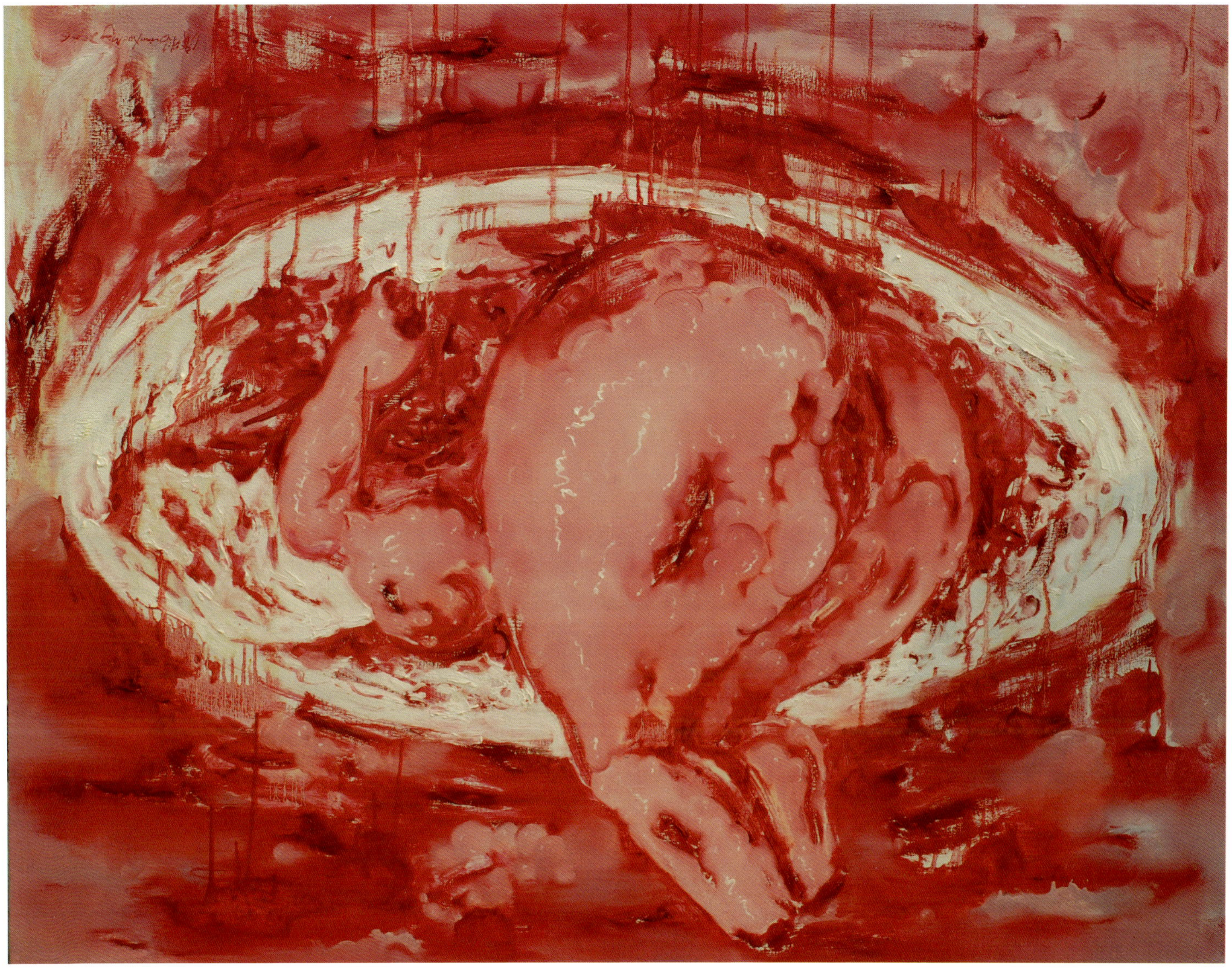

《欲餐15》
布面油画

The Lust for Food 15
Oil on canvas
110cm×140cm

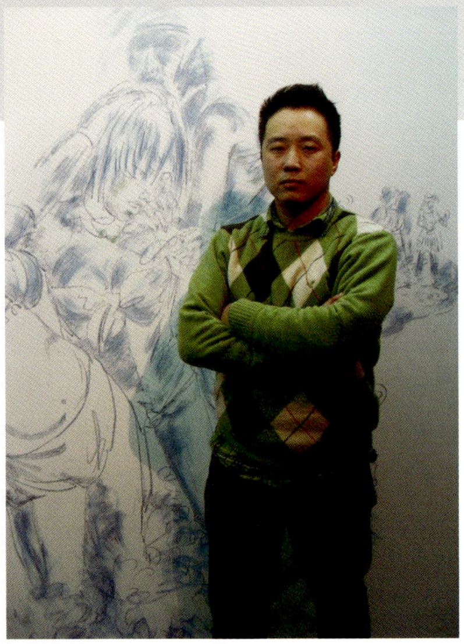

1971 Born in Chengdu, China
1998 Graduated from Sichuan Fine Arts Institute

Solo Exhibitions

1998 "Sacred Cat" Solo Exhibition of Shi Liu, Sichuan Fine Arts Institute and Southwest Normal University, Chongqing , China
2001 "Entangled" Solo Exhibition of Shi Liu, Chengdu, China

Group Exhibitions

1998 " Immigration" Art Exhibition, Sichuan Fine Arts Institute, Chongqing, China
1998 Exhibition of Changchun Chen & Shi Liu, Chongqing, China
2002 "Seeking" Experimental Art Show, Chengdu, China
2003 " Hometown" Art Exhibition, Sichuan Art Museum, Chengdu, China
2006 "Colour Red" Art Exhibition, 798 Millennium Art Gallery, Beijing, China
2006 " New Power · China" Contemporary Art Biennial, Shanghai, China

Collected by

Hong Kong Jing Feng Xuan Art Gallery
Millennium International Art Organization
Millennium Art Gallery
Fang Yin Art Centre

一九七一年生于中国成都
一九九八年毕业于四川美术学院

个展

一九九八年 《灵猫》 四川美术学院
西南师范学院
一九九九年 《灵猫》 中国成都
二〇〇一年 《纠缠》 中国成都

联展

一九九八年 《迁徙》 四川美术学院
一九九八年 《陈长春·刘石》 西南师范学院
二〇〇二年 《寻找》 实验艺术 中国成都巡展
二〇〇三年 《家园》 四川省美术馆 中国成都
二〇〇六年 《色空》 七九八千年时间画廊 中国北京
二〇〇六年 《红T画廊》 中国北京
二〇〇六年 《二〇〇六年新动力当代艺术双年展》 中国上海

收藏

香港季丰轩画廊
千年时间国际艺术管理机构
千年时间画廊
方音艺术中心

Shi Liu

刘石

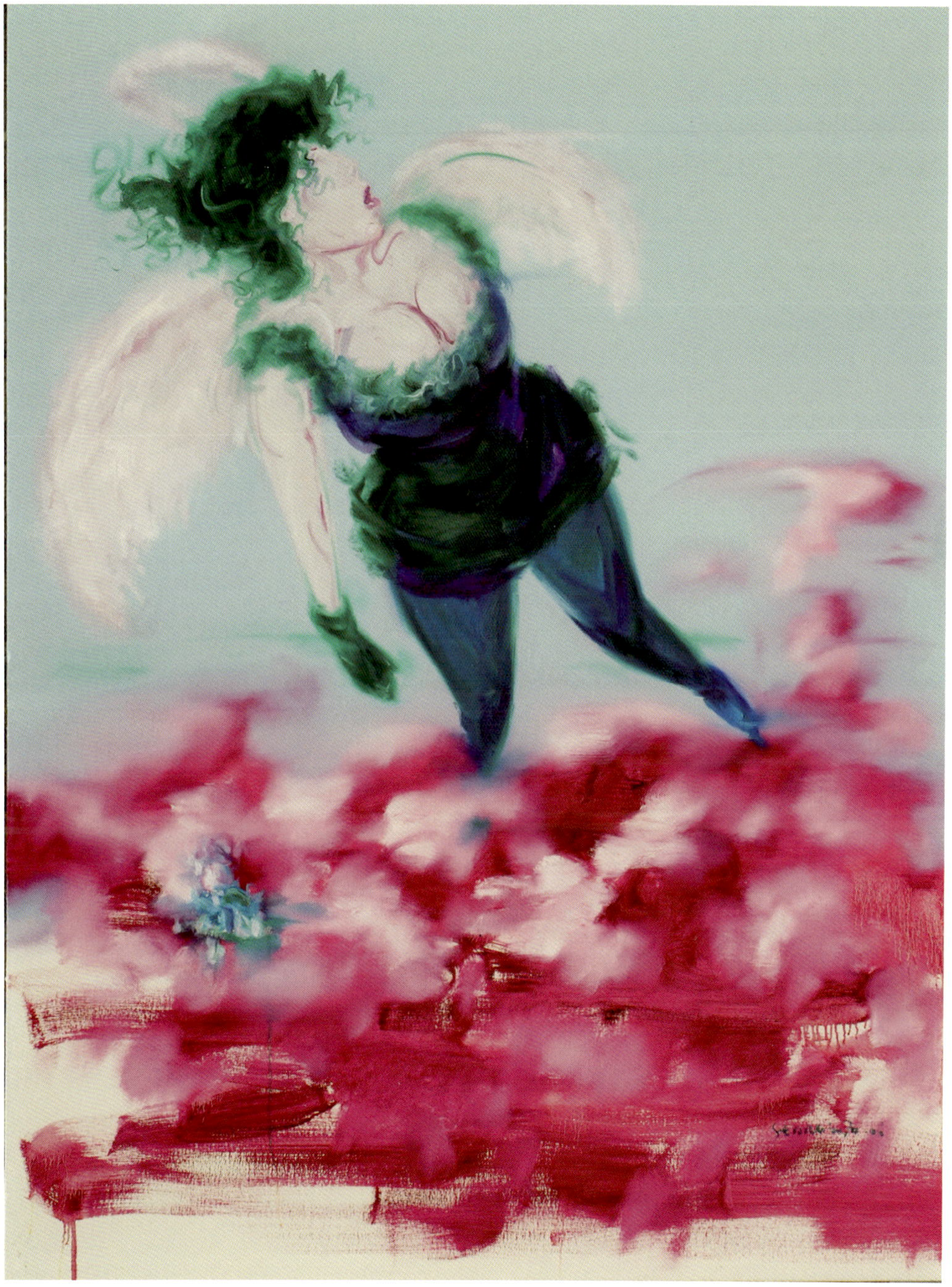

布面油画《玩偶80》

Puppet 80
Oil on canvas
200cm × 148cm

一九六八年生于中国四川
一九九二年毕业于四川美术学院获学士学位。现任乐山师院美术系副教授。

主要展览：

一九九二年 《四川美院油画作品展》 中国香港
一九九七年 《都市人格·1997刘兴涛油画个人展》 中国成都
一九九八年 《中国当代艺术文献资料展第五回》 中国重庆
一九九九年 《九十年代流行图象展》 中国上海
二〇〇一年 《一百个艺术家面孔》 中国南京
二〇〇二年 《四川省第二届青年美展》获优秀奖 中国成都
二〇〇三年 《四川省油画展》 中国成都
二〇〇三年 《第三届中国油画展》 中国北京
二〇〇四年 《四川省高校首届美术教师作品展》 中国成都
二〇〇五年参加 『趣味无穷』油画展 上海艺博画廊
二〇〇五年参加 『鲁艺杯』大赛，获学术奖 鲁迅美术学院

主要发表：

油画作品曾发于《美术》、《艺术家》、《美术界》、《93中国美术家》、《都市人格与当代艺术》、《艺术界》、《艺术当代》、《东方艺术》、《全国高等美术教育教师作品集》等专业刊物。

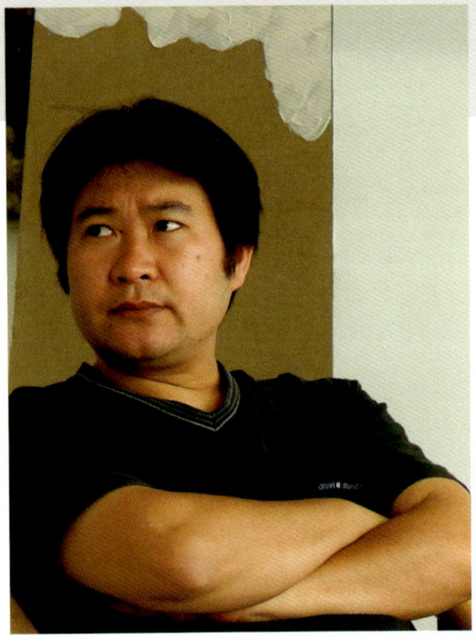

1968 Born in Sichuan，China
1992 Graduated from Sichuan Fine Arts Institute with a Bachelor’s Degree
Currently Associate Professor in Fine Arts Department, Leshan Teachers College

Exhibitions

1992 Oil Painting Exhibition of Sichuan Fine Arts Institute, Hong Kong, China
1997 “City Personalities” Solo Exhibition of Xintao Liu, Chengdu, China
1998 Contemporary Art Documentary Exhibition (5) Account for Contemporary Art in the 1990s, Chongqing, China
1999 1990s Popular Images Art Exhibition, Shanghai, China
2001 “Faces of the 100 Artists” Art Exhibition, Nanjing, China
2002 2nd Sichuan Youth Art Exhibition, awarded with a Prize for Excellence, Chengdu, China
2003 3rd China National Oil Painting Exhibition, Beijing, China
2003 Sichuan Oil Painting Exhibition, Chengdu, China
2004 1st Sichuan Teachers’ Works Exhibition of Fine Arts Academies, Chengdu, China
2005 “Lu Xun Art Cup” Grand Competition, awarded with an Academic Prize, Lu Xun Fine Arts Academy
2005 “Endless Interest” Oil Painting Exhibition, Shanghai Yi Bo Gallery, Shanghai, China

The main works and issues:

The main oil painting works once were published in professional publications, such as Art, Artist, Fine Arts Field, Chinese Artists in 1993, City Personality and Contemporary Art, Art Field, Art Contemporary, Eastern Art, National Album of Fine Arts College Teachers , etc.

Xintao Liu

刘芯（兴）涛

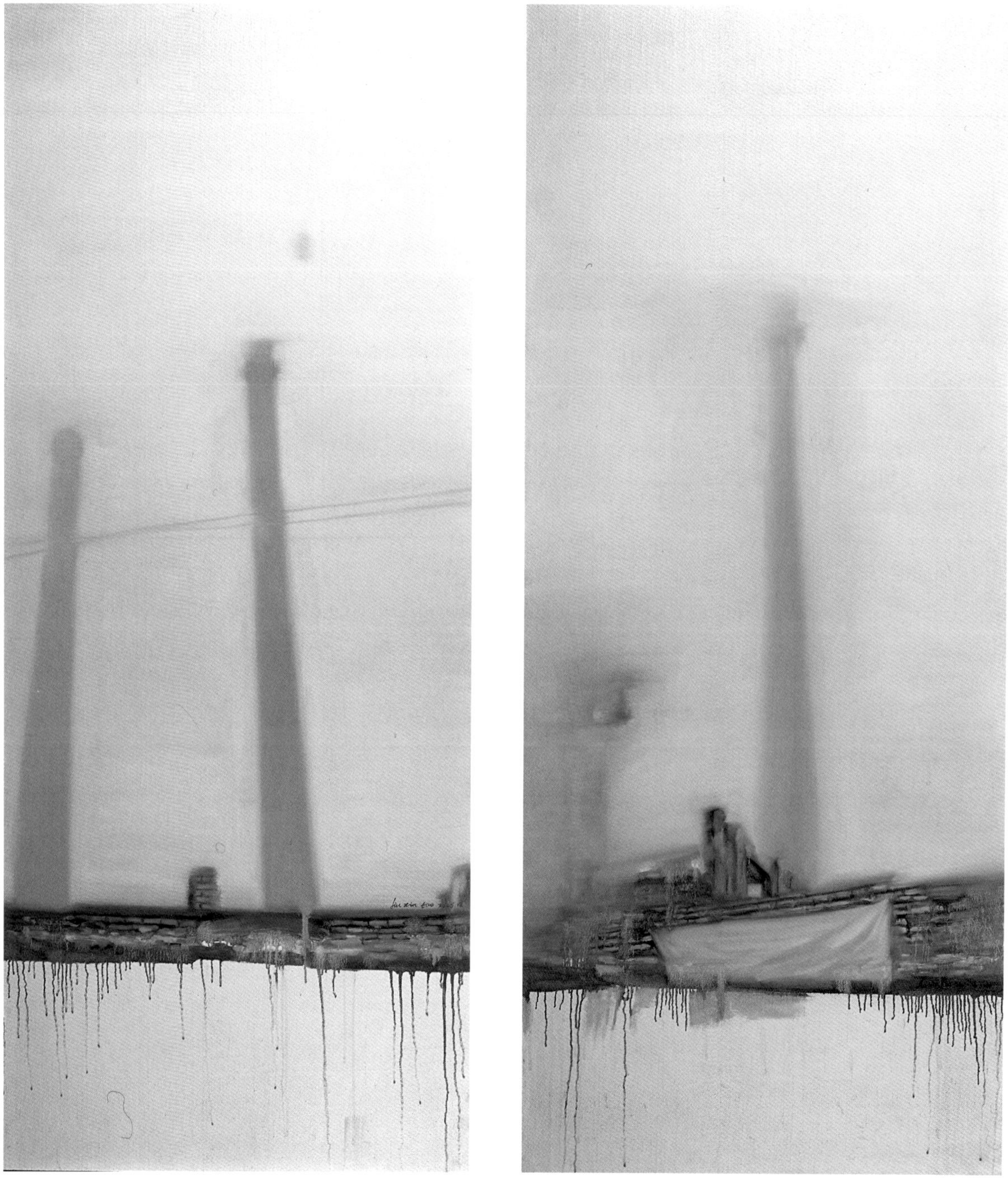

《逝去的风景》
布面油画

The Lost Sceneries
Oil on canvas
180cm × 75cm

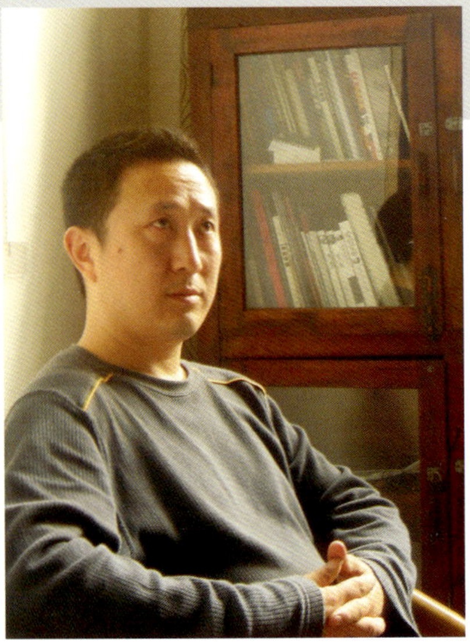

1968 Born in November
1991 Graduated from Sichuan Fine Arts Institute
Currently lives and works in Chengdu

Solo Exhibitions
2006 "Prison" Series, Vanessa Art Link Gallery

Group Exhibitions
2006 "Changed Pictures", Shanghai Art Museum
2006 "Drip · Prison · Touch", Beijing Shengman Gallery
2006 New Power Biennale of Shanghai, Yuangong Art Museum

Collected by:
2006 Yuangong Art Museum, Shanghai
2006 Qinghe Art Museum, Nanjing

生于一九六八年十一月
一九九一年毕业于四川美术学院
现工作和居住在成都

个展：
二〇〇六年十一月 《囚》系列 北京华艺沙艺术中心

群展：
二〇〇六年十二月 《变异的图像》 上海美术馆
二〇〇六年九月 《滴、囚、触》 北京圣曼画廊
二〇〇六年九月 《新动力上海双年展》 上海原弓美术馆

收藏：
二〇〇六年九月 上海原弓美术馆
二〇〇六年六月 南京青和美术馆

Jie Luo

罗杰

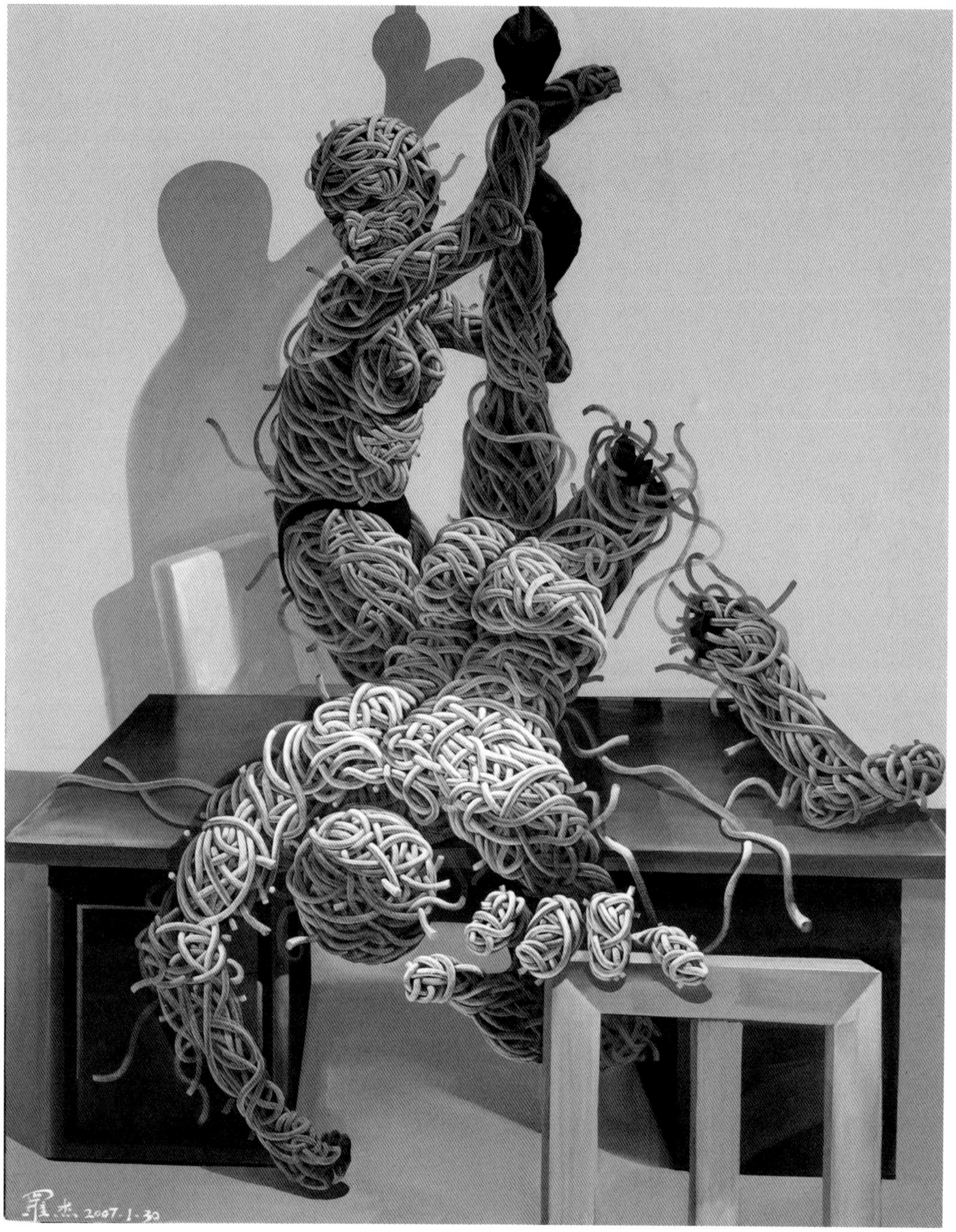

布面油画
《囚NO.35》

Prison No. 35
Oil on canvas
165cm × 210cm

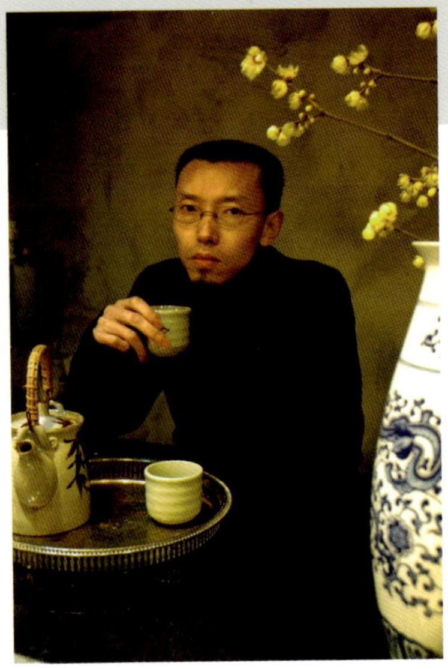

一九七〇年生于中国四川
一九九六年毕业于四川美术学院油画系，获学士学位。
二〇〇六年『新动力』上海北京双年展。

1970 Born in Sichuan，China
1996 Graduated from Oil Painting Department, Sichuan Fine Arts Institute with a Bachelor’s Degree

Exhibitions
2006 1st “New Power · China” Contemporary Art Biennial, Beijing and Shanghai

YUqi Luo

罗玉其

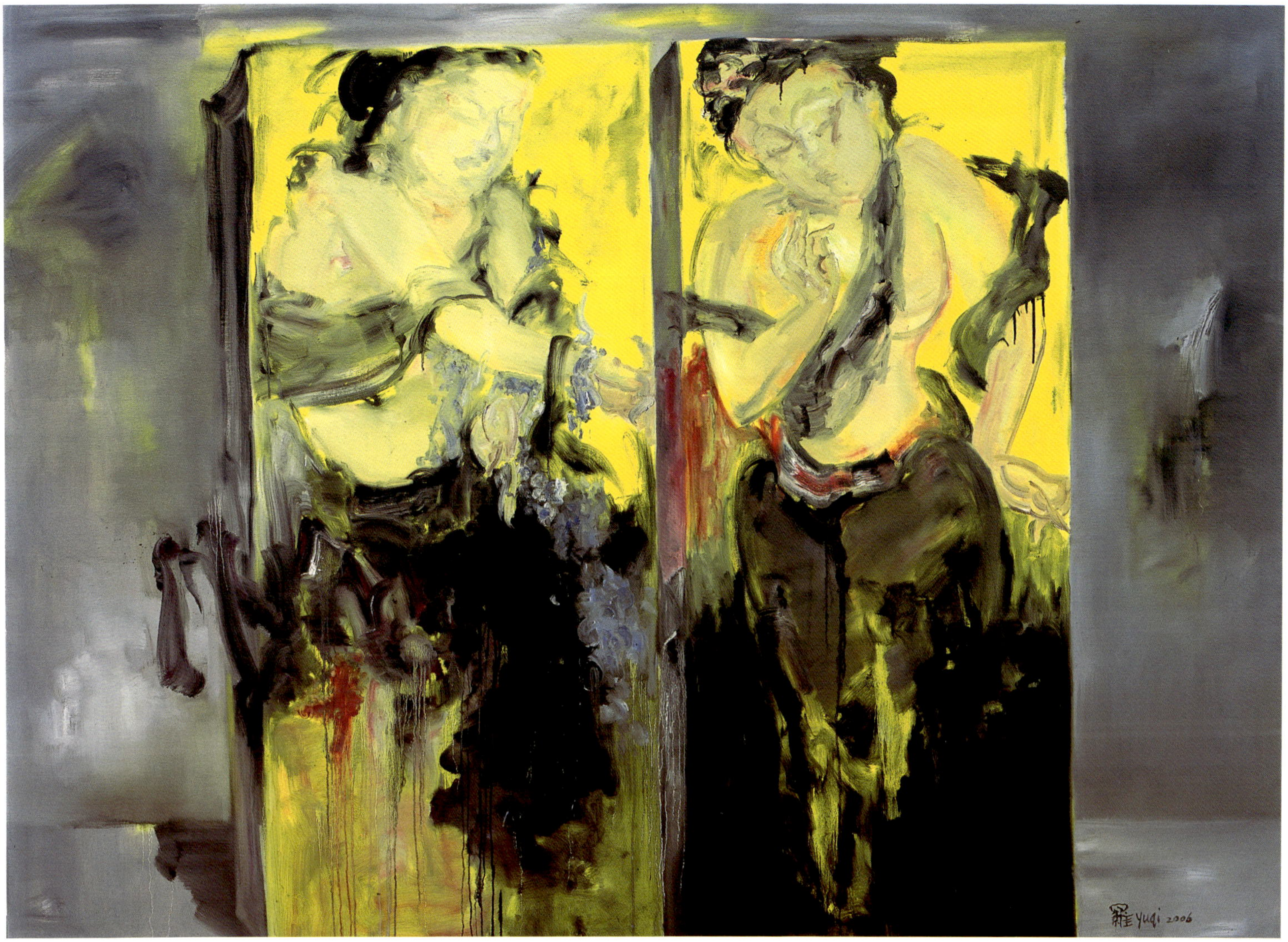

《旅居1》
布面油画

Residing abroad 1
Oil on canvas
280cm×180.5cm

生于中国四川
一九九六年毕业于四川美术学院油画系
二○○○年结业于中央美术学院油画进修班
二○○三年考入四川大学艺术学院攻读硕士研究生
现任教于四川音乐学院

主要展览：
二○○一年 油画《夜》『四川省第五届体育美展』 四川美术馆
二○○二年 油画《惊吓的鸽子》『纪念毛主席延安讲话60周年全国美术大展』 中国美术馆
二○○三年 油画《聚会》『携手新世纪第三届中国油画展』 中国美术馆
二○○五年 油画《战将系列》参加『宽窄景艺术沙龙油画展』徐悲鸿艺术交流中心
二○○六年 油画《马的寓言系列》参加《首届（2006）『新动力·中国』当代艺术双年展》上海原弓美术馆
《首届（2006）『新动力·中国』当代艺术双年展北京邀请展》上海原弓美术馆 北京TS1『宋庄壹号』当代艺术中心
《（2007）『新动力·中国』艺术家提名展》上海美术馆原弓艺术机构

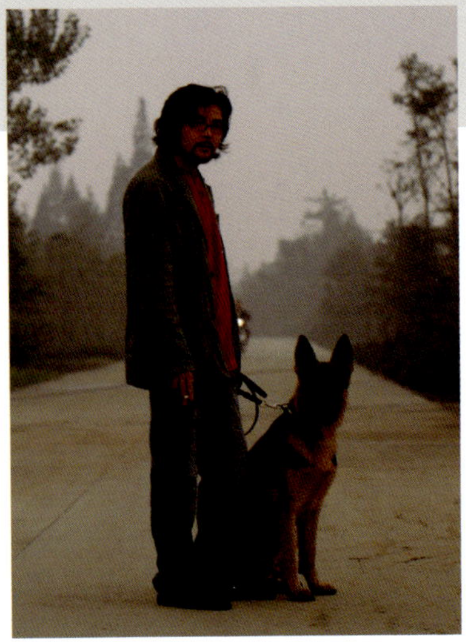

Born in Sichuan, China
1996 Graduated from Oil Painting Department, Sichuan Fine Arts Institute
2000 Graduated from Oil Painting Research Class, China Central Academy of Fine Arts
2003 Entered Fine Arts Academy of Sichuan University, tutored by Professor Conglin Cheng
Currently teaches in Sichuan Conservatory of Music

Exhibitions

2001 Night attended 5th Sichuan Sport Fine Arts Exhibition, Sichuan Art Museum
2002 The Scared Dove attended National Fine Arts Exhibition in honor of the 60th Anniversary of Chairman Mao' Speech at Yan' an Conference, China National Art Museum
2003 Party attended "Hand in Hand in the New Century" 3rd China National Oil Painting Exhibition, China National Art Museum
2005 Warriors series attended "Wide • Narrow" Landscape Oil Painting Salon Exhibition, Xu Bei Hong Arts Exchange Centre
2006 "New Power • China" Nominative Exhibition 2007, Shanghai Art Museum and Shanghai Yuan Gong G Art Museum
2006 The Invited Exhibition of the 1st "New Power • China" Contemporary Arts Biennial, Shanghai Y&G Art Museum, Beijing TS1 Contemporary Art Centre
2006 The Legend of the Horse series attended 1st "New Power • China" Contemporary Art Biennial, Shanghai YuanGong Art Museum

Guangping Qiu

邱光平

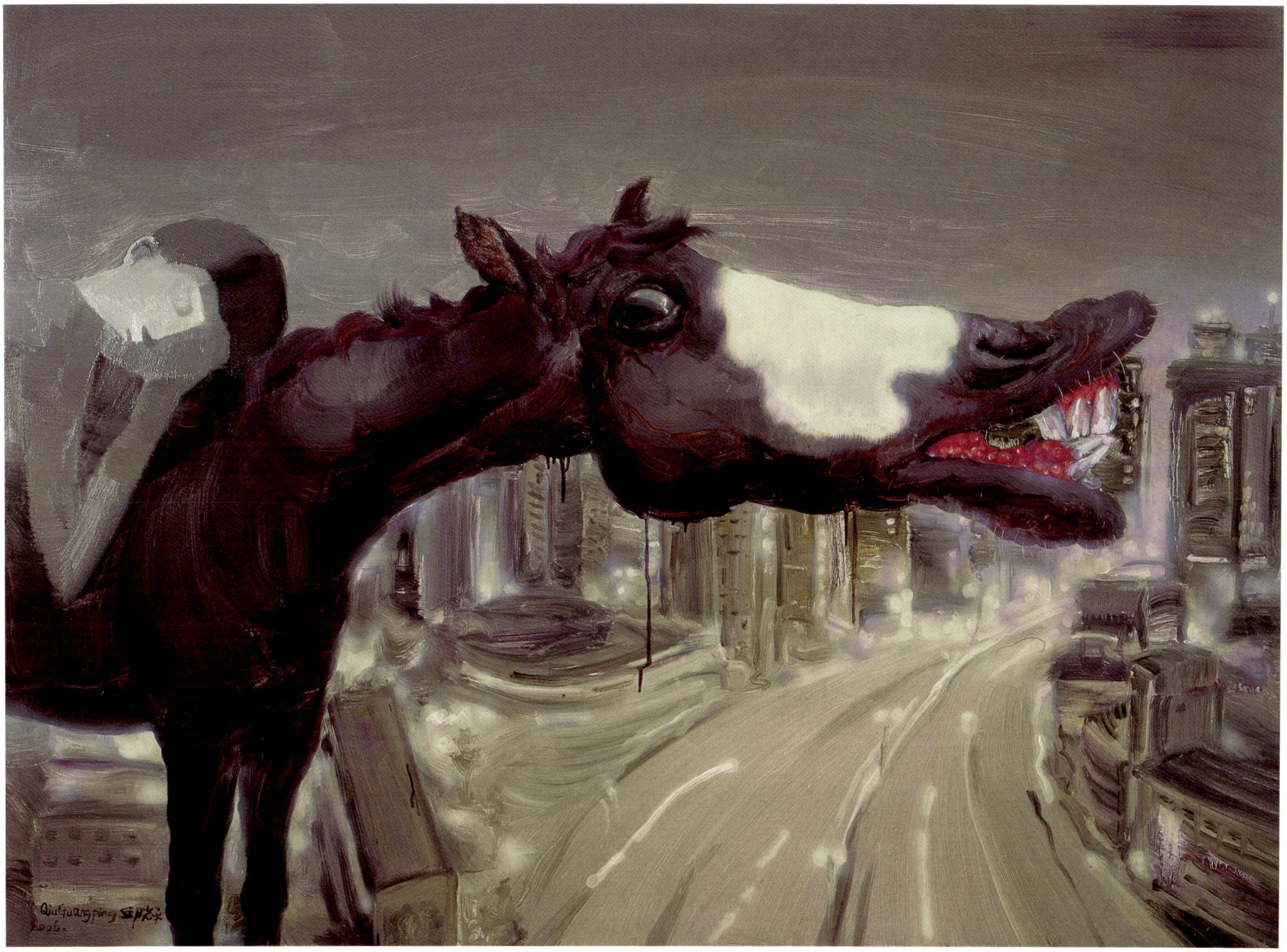

《不夜城》
布面油画

The SleepLess City
Oil on canvas
150cm×110cm

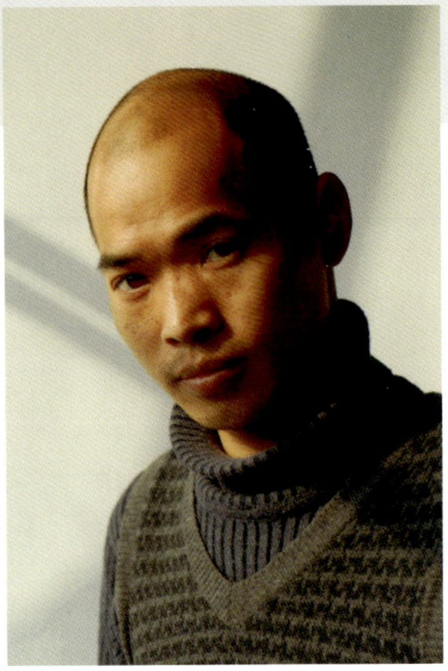

1974 Born in Sichuan，China
1996 Studied in Oil Painting Department, Sichuan Fine Arts Institute
2003 Studied in Oil Painting Department of Sichuan University for a Master’s Degree，directed by Mr. Chonglin Cheng

Exhibitions

1999 Nokia Invited Art Exhibition (Gold Prize winner)
2002 Glorious City Art Salon Exhibition
2002 New Starting Point I and New Starting Point II attended Sichuan Youth Art Exhibition
New Starting Point III attended Sichuan Young Talent and Their Lately Works Exhibition
2003 Chongqing Memories after going to Xi’an attended 9th China National Fine Arts Exhibition
2003-2006 “Season Spring” Oil Painting Salon Exhibitions of Sichuan

一九七四年出生于中国重庆
一九九六年考入四川美术学院油画系
二〇〇三年考入四川大学攻读油画研究生
一九九八年油画创作『到西安几天后回忆重庆』入选第九届美展
一九九九年油画创作『未来都市』获诺基亚艺术邀请展中国赛区金奖
二〇〇二年油画创作『新起点一』『新起点二』入选四川省新人新作展
油画创作『新起点三』入选四川省青年美展
二〇〇三年-二〇〇六年参加四川油画艺术沙龙系列展

Feng Tian

田丰

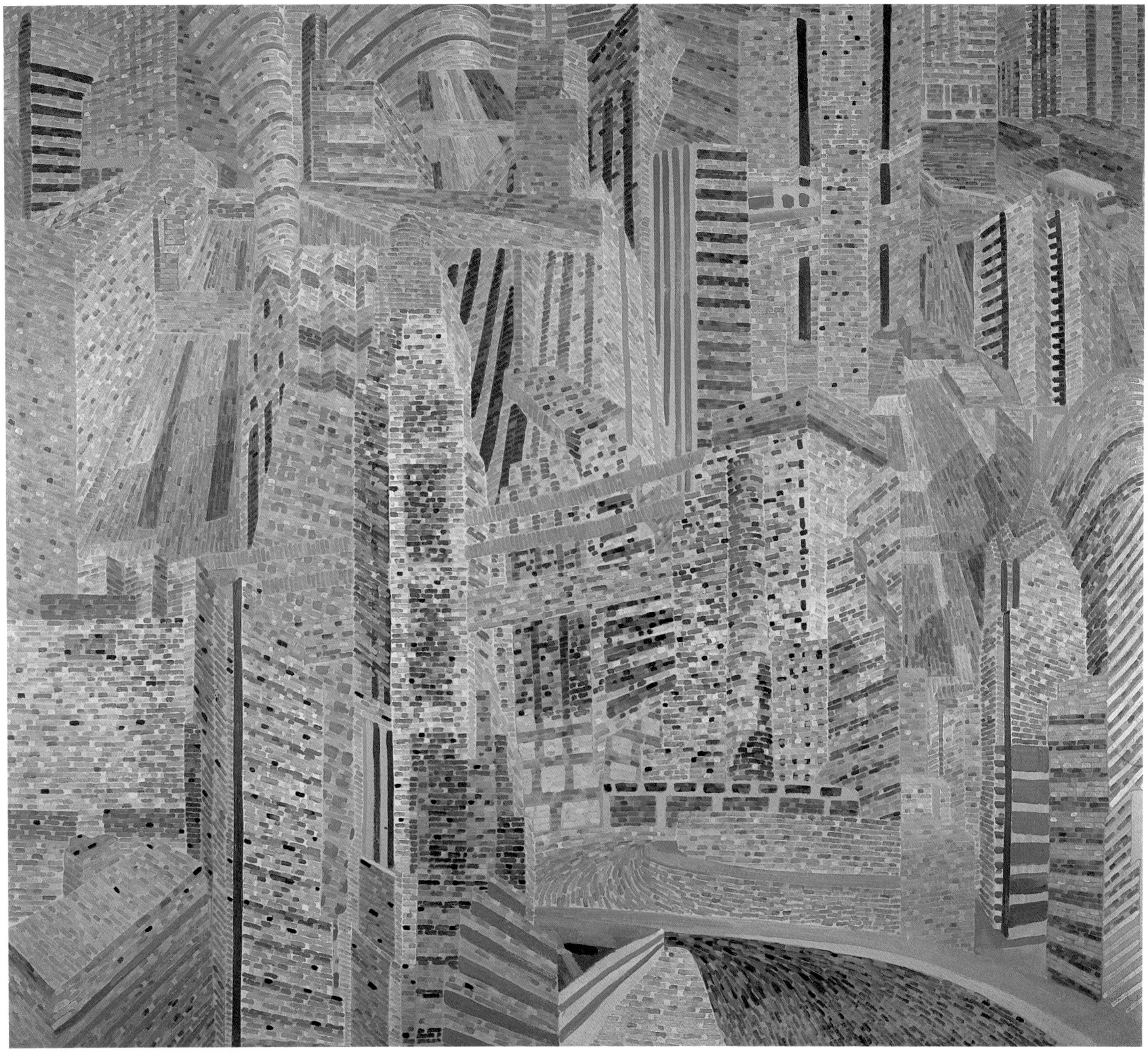

《城市印象》
布面油画

City impression
Oil on canvas
175cm×150cm

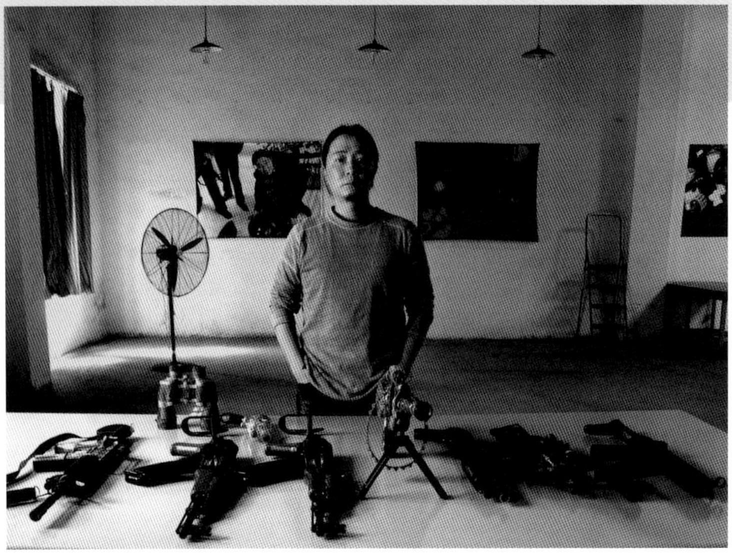

1993 Graduated from Oil Painting Department, Sichuan Fine Arts Institute

Recent Exhibitions

1995 1st Chengdu Oil Painting Exhibition, Chengdu, China
1996 2nd Chengdu Oil Painting Exhibition, Chengdu, China
2001 "Eclosion" Art Exhibition, Chengdu, China
2002 "Seeking" Contemporary Art Exhibition, Chengdu, China
2003 "135M135" Contemporary Art Exhibition, Sichuan Art Museum
2006 "156M156" Contemporary Art Exhibition, Sichuan Art Museum

一九九三年毕业于四川美院油画系
一九九五年五月『成都首届油画展』 中国成都
一九九六年10月『成都第二届油画展』 中国北京
二〇〇一年七月『羽化』艺术展 中国成都
二〇〇二年九月『巡找』当代艺术巡回展 中国成都
二〇〇三年四月『135M135』当代艺术展 四川美术馆
二〇〇六年10月『156M156』当代艺术展 四川美术馆

Chengdian Wu

吴承典

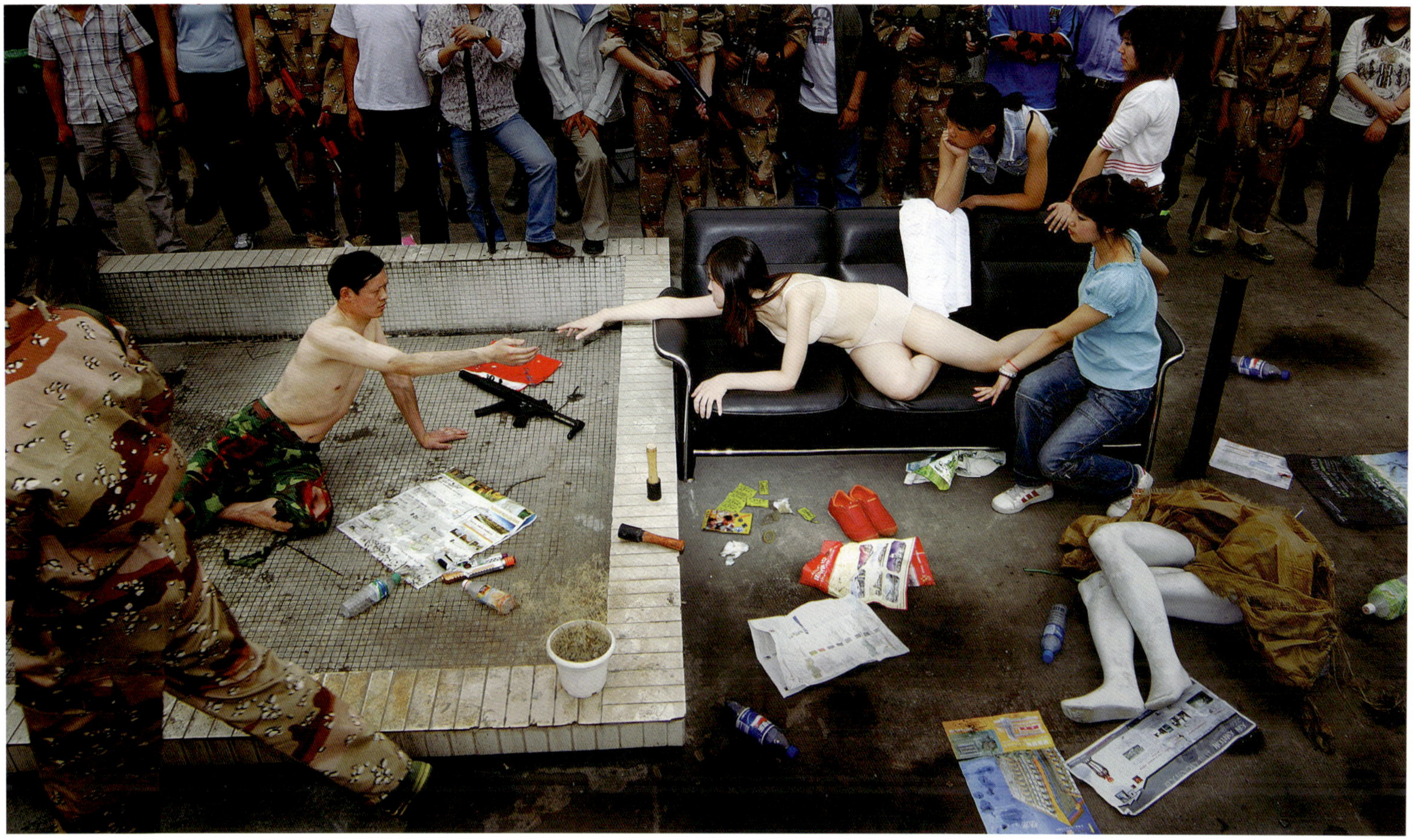

图像《创世纪》

Genesis
Photograph
60cm × 102cm

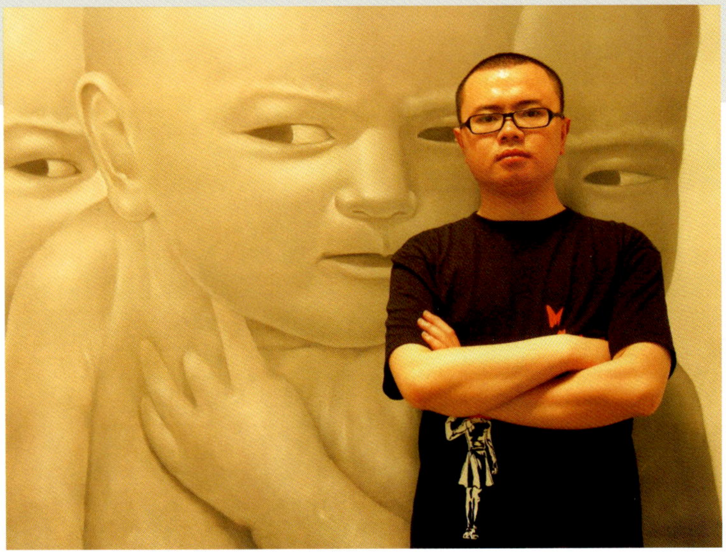

1976 Born in Sichuan, China
1996 Studied at No.1 Studio of Sichuan Fine Arts Institute
2000 Graduated from Sichuan Fine Arts Institute with a Bachelor' s Degree
2003 Graduated from Sichuan Fine Arts Institute with a Master' s Degree
Currently lives in Chengdu

Exhibitions

1997 9th China National Fine Arts Exhibition in Chongqing Area, Chongqing, China
2000 "Nokia · Paradise for Imagination" Fine Arts Exhibition, Beijing, China
2002 "Experimental Art Education" Exhibition, Chongqing Art Museum, Chongqing, China
2003 1st Oil Painting Biennial of Chongqing, Chongqing, China
2004 1st Sichuan Teachers' Works Exhibition of Colleges, Chengdu, China
2005 "Endless Interest" Fine Arts Exhibition, Shanghai Yi Bo Art Gallery, Shanghai, China

Collected by

Some of the works were collected by Sichuan Fine Arts Institute and Contemporary Artists magazine, etc. and published in China Oil Painting, Jiangsu Art Periodical, Contemporary Artists, Art Garden, Album of Excellent Works by College teachers issued by Contemporary Art and Design

一九七六年出生于中国四川。
一九九六年进入四川美术学院油画系第一工作室学习。
二〇〇〇年七月毕业并获学士学位。
二〇〇三年七月四川美术学院油画系研究生毕业获硕士学位。现工作生活于成都。

展览

一九九七年第九届全国美展重庆市展　中国重庆
二〇〇〇年诺基亚『想象力的乐园』美展　中国北京
二〇〇二年重庆美术馆开馆系列展『实验的艺术教育』展　中国重庆
二〇〇三年重庆市首届油画展　中国重庆
二〇〇四年四川省高校教师作品展　中国成都
二〇〇五年『趣味无穷展』，上海艺博画廊　中国上海

作品被四川美术学院美术馆、《当代美术家》等收藏。作品曾发表于《中国油画》，《江苏画刊》，《美苑》，《当代美术家》，高校教师优秀作品集《当代美术与设计》等期刊杂志。

Yongkang Xu

许永康

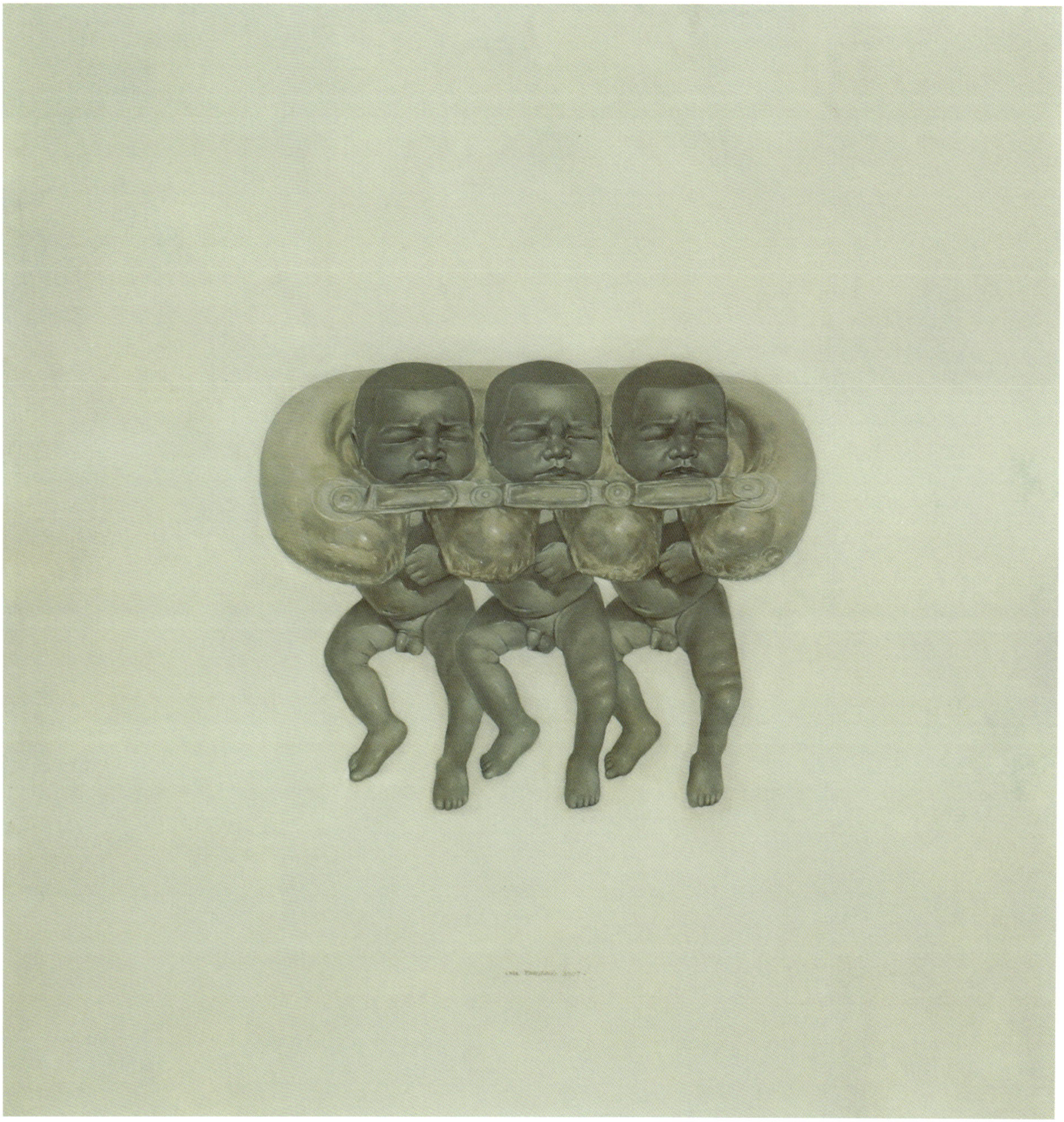

《美丽新世界1》
布面油画

The Beautiful New World1
Oil on canvas
200cm×180cm

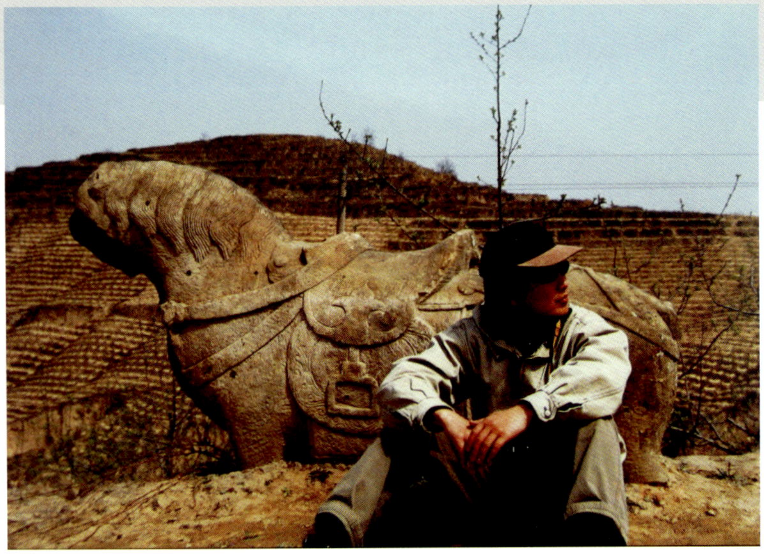

1987 Graduated from Sichuan Fine Arts Institute
Currently teaches in Teachers College of Chengdu University

Exhibitions

1988 Sichuan Oil Painting Exhibition, Chengdu
1989 1st China Southwest Contemporary Art Exhibition,
1993 Sichuan Oil Painting Exhibition, Chengdu
1996 Chengdu Oil Painting Exhibition, China National Art Museum, Beijing
2003 3rd Annual Exhibition of China Oil Painting Association
2004 10th National Oil Painting Exhibition in Sichuan Area
2005 10 Years Treasure Collection Show, Ya Feng Gallery

一九八七年毕业于四川美术学院
一九八八年十月参加四川省油画展
一九八九年参加首届西南现代艺术展
一九九三年参加四川省油画展
一九九六年参加北京中国美术馆『成都油画展』
二〇〇三年参加中国油画学会第三届油画年展
二〇〇四年参加全国十届油画四川油画展
二〇〇五年参加雅风画廊十年典藏展
现就职于成都大学师范学院。

Chunsheng Yang

杨春生

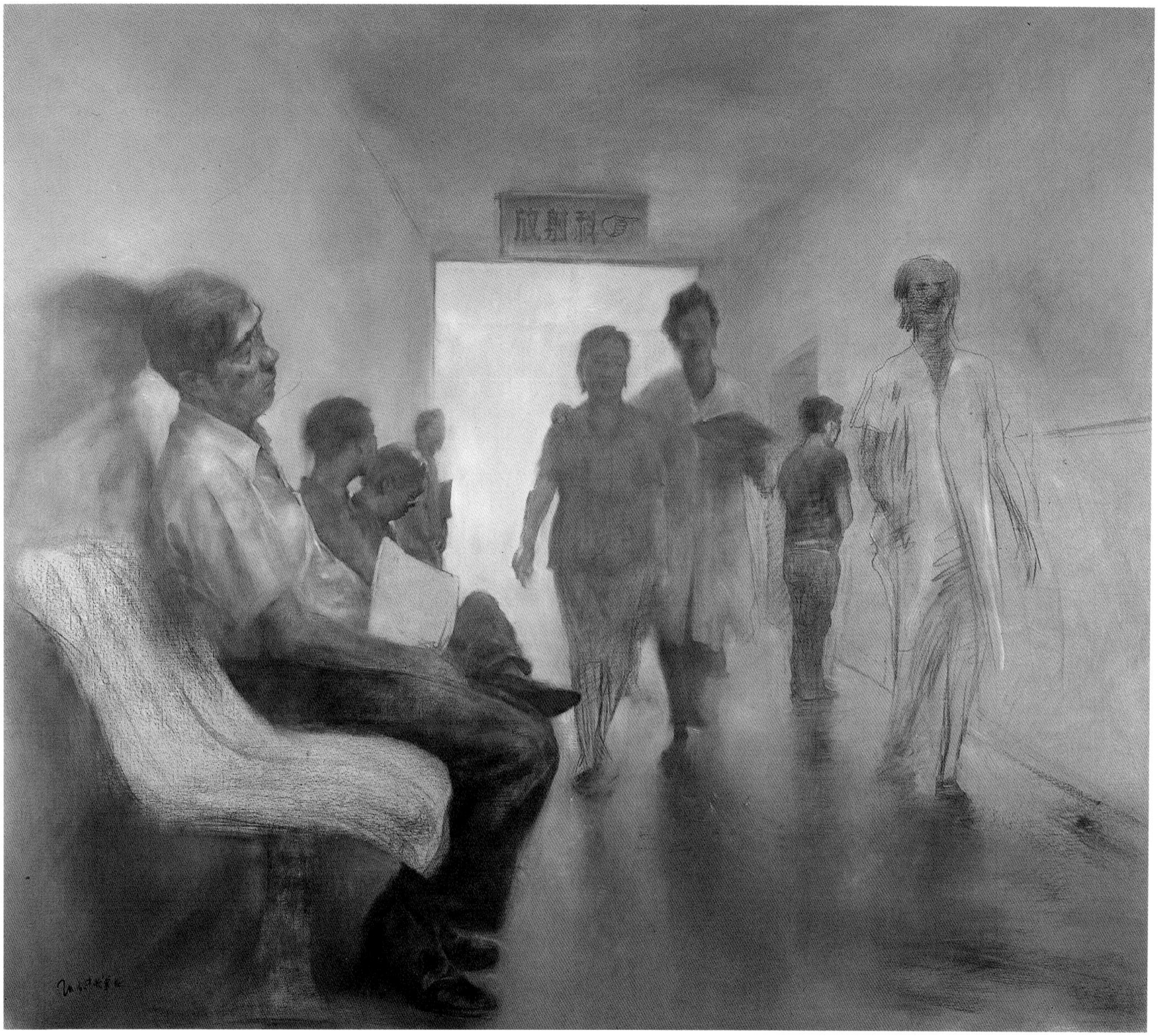

《蓉城游记-放射走廊》
布面油画

Wander at Chengdu at
The Corridor outside The Radiation Centre
Oil on canvas
189cm × 170cm

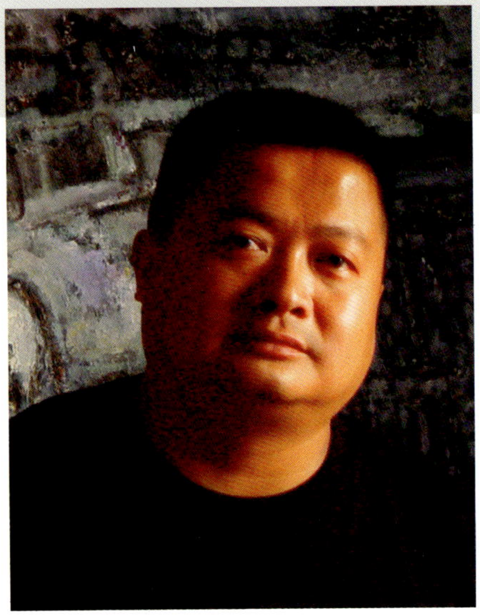

1967 Born in Sichuan， China
1990 Graduated from Oil Painting Department, Sichuan Fine Arts Institute with a Bachelor's Degree
Currently teaches in Painting Department of Fine Arts Academy, Sichuan University
Associate Professor of Fine Arts Academy of Sichuan University
Tutor in Oil Painting
Vice Director of New Fine Arts Research Centre

一九六七年生于中国四川。
一九九〇年毕业于四川美术学院油画系，获学士学位。
一九九六年至今任教于四川大学艺术学院绘画系。
现为四川大学艺术学院副教授、油画硕士研究生导师、四川大学新艺术研究中心副主任。

Hanmei Yang

杨寒梅

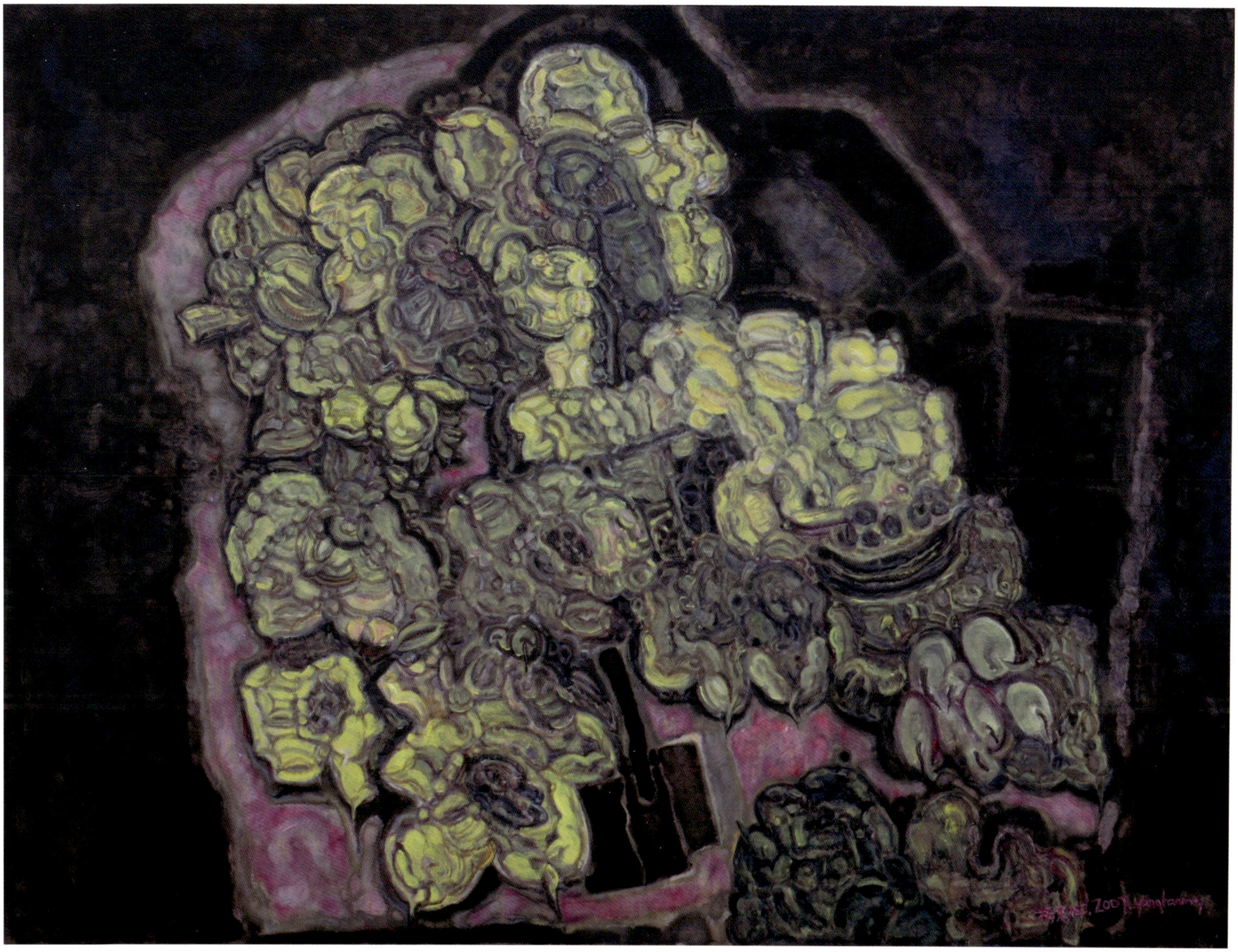

《花1》
布面油画

Flowers1
Oil on canvas
150cm×200cm

一九七〇年生于中国四川

一九九八—二〇〇〇年四川教育学院油画班

二〇〇〇年8月入驻『浓园』建立工作室

个展：

二〇〇二年『关于龙』 羚羊画廊 中国成都

二〇〇〇年『画布上的音乐』 四川音乐学院 中国成都

主要展览：

二〇〇三年『灰中的黑』携手新世纪四川暨成都油画大展 中国成都

二〇〇二年『龙·金版』『龙·银版』四川第二界青年油画展 中国成都

二〇〇一年『吹笛人·午后』『鹧鸪山之一』新美国际画廊 中国台湾

二〇〇〇年『俯冲·黄』『俯冲·绿』四川风景油画展 中国成都

一九九八年『吹笛人·蓝夜』『江苏画刊』首界『中国艺术双年展』 中国南京 加拿大多伦多

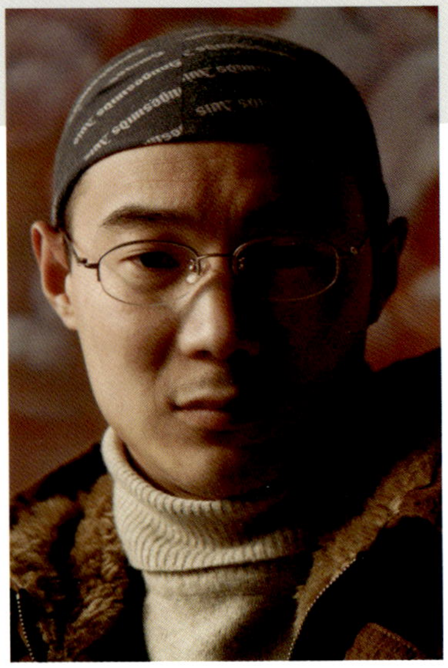

1970 Born in Chengdu, China

2000 Graduated from Oil Painting Class of Sichuan College of Education

2006 Set up the studio at Chengdu International Nongyuan Arts Creating Centre

Solo Exhibition:

2002 "About Dragon" Art Exhibition, Linyang Gallery, Chengdu, China

2000 " Music on Canvas" Oil Painting Exhibition, Sichuan Conservatory of Music, Chengdu, China

Other Exhibition experiences:

2003 Black in Gray attended " Embracing the New Century" Oil Painting Exhibition, Chengdu, China

2002 Dragon • Gold Edition and Dragon • Sliver Edition attended 2nd Youth Oil Painting Exhibition, Chengdu, China

2001 A Man Playing the Flute • Afternoon and Zhegu Mountain I attended Xinmei International Gallery, Taiwan, China

2000 "Dive · Yellow" and "Dive · Green" Sichuan Landscape Oil Painting Exhibition, Chengdu

1998 A Man Playing the Flute • Blue Night attended 1st China Fine Arts Biennial, China, Toronto and Canada

Guoqiang Zhang

张国强

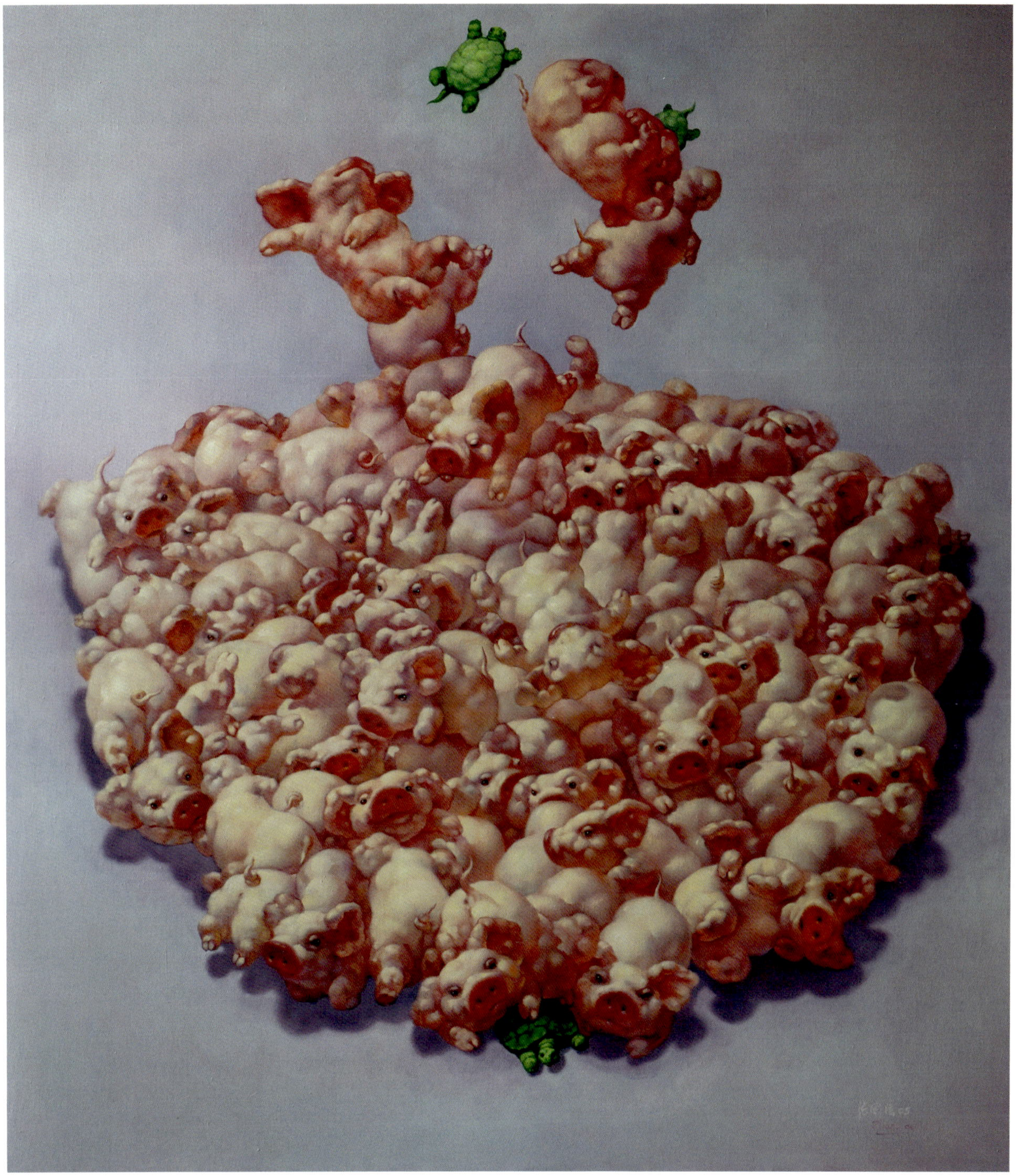

布面油画《肉系列04-5》

Meat series04-5
Oil on canvas
180cm×155cm

参展作品名单

List of works in the exhibition

艺术家：曹阳
作品名称：门影NO. 35
材质：布面油画
尺寸：120cm×120cm

艺术家：程翔
作品名称：出窍
材质：铸铜
尺寸：90cm×22cm×50cm

艺术家：陈硕
作品名称：快速发展-婴儿系列
材质：陶
尺寸：32.5cm×18cm×9.4cm

艺术家：刁毅
作品名称：夜宴一
材质：布面油画
尺寸：150cm×200cm

艺术家：韩情
作品名称：街灯2002NO. 12
材质：布面油画
尺寸：145cm×115cm

艺术家：黄明进
作品名称：在·不在10
材质：布面油画
尺寸：200cm×150cm

Yang Cao
The vision of the Doors NO.35
Oil on canvas
120cm×120cm
Courtesy of the Yang Cao

Xiang Cheng
The Outflow of the Souls
Copper
90cm×22cm×50cm
Courtesy of the Xiang Cheng

Shuo Chen
The Fast Development- Baby Series
Ceramics
32.5cm×18cm×9.4cm
Courtesy of the Shuo Chen

Yi Diao
Night Banquet 1
Oil on canvas
150cm×200cm
Courtesy of the Yi Diao

Qing Han
Street Lights 2002 NO.12
Oil on canvas
145cm×115cm
Courtesy of the Qing Han

Mingjin Huang
To be or not to be NO.10
Oil on canvas
200cm×150cm
Courtesy of the Mingjin Huang

艺术家：蒋晶
作品名称：遗忘时光
材质：影像作品
尺寸：100cm×75cm

Jing Jiang
The Lost Time and Space
Photograph
100cm×75cm
Courtesy of the Jing Jiang

艺术家：蒋鹏
作品名称：消灭一切害虫3
材质：布面油画
尺寸：170cm×150cm

Peng Jiang
Kill all the Pests 3
Oil on canvas
170cm×150cm
Courtesy of the Peng Jiang

艺术家：李貌
作品名称：见惯不惊
材质：布面油画
尺寸：170cm×155cm

Mao Li
Confronting Without Excitement
Oil on canvas
170cm×155cm
Courtesy of the Mao Li

艺术家：廉学洺
作品名称：欲餐15
材质：布面油画
尺寸：110cm×140cm

Xueming Lian
The Lust for Food 15
Oil on canvas
110cm×140cm
Courtesy of the Xueming Lian

艺术家：刘石
作品名称：玩偶80
材质：布面油画
尺寸：200cm×148cm

Shi Liu
Puppet 80
Oil on canvas
200cm×148cm
Courtesy of the Shi Liu

艺术家：刘芯（兴）涛
作品名称：逝去的风景
材质：布面油画
尺寸：180cm×75cm

Xintao Liu
The Lost Sceneries
Oil on canvas
180cm×75cm
Courtesy of the Xintao Liu

艺术家：罗杰
作品名称：囚NO. 35
材质：布面油画
尺寸：165cm×210cm

艺术家：罗玉其
作品名称：旅居1
材质：布面油画
尺寸：280cm×180cm

艺术家：邱光平
作品名称：不夜城
材质：布面油画
尺寸：150cm×110cm

艺术家：田丰
作品名称：城市印象
材质：布面油画
尺寸：170cm×150cm

艺术家：吴承典
作品名称：创世纪
材质：影像作品
尺寸：60cm×102cm

艺术家：许永康
作品名称：美丽新世界1
材质：布面油画
尺寸：200cm×180cm

Jie Luo
Prison No. 35
Oil on canvas
160cm×210cm
Courtesy of the Jie Luo

Yuqi Luo
Residing abroad 1
Oil on canvas
280cm×180.5cm
Courtesy of the Yuqi Luo

Guangping Qiu
The Sleepless City
Oil on canvas
150cm×110cm
Courtesy of the Guangping Qiu

Feng Tian
City Impression
Oil on canvas
175cm×150cm
Courtesy of the Feng Tian

Chengdian Wu
Genesis
Photograph
60cm×102cm
Courtesy of the Chengdian Wu

Yongkang Xu
The Beautiful New World 1
Oil on canvas
200cm×180cm
Courtesy of the Yongkang Xu

艺术家：杨春生
作品名称：蓉城游记-放射走廊
材质：布面油画
尺寸：189cm×170cm

艺术家：杨寒梅
作品名称：花1
材质：布面油画
尺寸：150cm×200cm

艺术家：张国强
作品名称：肉系列04-5
材质：布面油画
尺寸：180cm×155cm

Chunsheng Yang
Wander at Chengdu - at The Corridor outside The Radiation Centre
Oil on canvas
189cm×170cm
Courtesy of the Chunsheng Yang

Hanmei Yang
Flowers 1
Oil on canvas
150cm×200cm
Courtesy of the Hanmei Yang

Guoqiang Zhang
Meat series 04-5
Oil on canvas
180cm×155cm
Courtesy of the Guoqiang Zhang